Choose to Thrive

Conquering Your Inner Conflicts

Debbie Luxton

Choose to Thrive

Conquering Your Inner Conflicts

Debbie Luxton
www.debbieluxton.com

Published by One Life to THRIVE, LLC
www.onelifetothrive.org

Choose to Thrive

Cover Design: The Writing King
Interior Design: The Writing King
Publisher: One Life to THRIVE, LLC
Editor: Mary Busha, Your Time to Write
Creative Consultant: The Writing King -
https://www.theghostwritingking.com

Library of Congress Catalog Number:

ISBN: 978-0-9985042-3-0

First Edition
Printed in USA.

Dedication

My dedication goes out to Jesus first. Without Him, this book would never be possible.

To my grandmother who had great influence on my life.
I can't wait to hug her in heaven.

To my mother for her courage and determination.
It wasn't easy being a young, single mother in the days when she was raising me.

To my husband for his patient wisdom and for always believing in me.

To all my children who have suffered and rejoiced through my good and bad decisions in life and in the awakening of who God created me to be.

To my Aunt Sandy, Uncle Wayne and Aunt Kathy who loved me regardless of my faults.

To the many other family members and friends who have inspired and supported me on this journey called life.

Table of Contents

Introduction

High-achieving women (some might call us strong-willed) help advance the world. Able-bodied, we take on a lot because we can. Others look to us for guidance and direction because we are natural leaders. We hold positions of authority and we are responsible for moving many things forward. The world is a better place because we are in it. Mostly.

I'm grateful that I can *freely* admit that I am a high-achieving woman. I've been quite proud of that throughout my life, so it's an easy admission. I am also grateful that I can say I have many great characteristics that are both my assets and my weaknesses. What is hard to admit is that I allowed my weaknesses (better known as character defects) to make my life miserable for many years. Really miserable. And the misery didn't affect only me. That's been the toughest thing of all to live with.

I am the mother of five, grandmother of ten and great maw-maw of one. I retired from a 30-year corporate career in 2008. I miss it. I loved the work I was doing, and more than that, I loved helping people be the best they can be. Since retiring, I have served in multiple volunteer leadership roles at my church and in local community organizations. I have served on a state-

Introduction

wide board of directors, as well as a local Board of Directors for a national organization. These roles have afforded me opportunities to use my organizational and teaming skills as well as fulfill my desire to give back and continue to help others be the best they can be. In 2010, I became an entrepreneur – a life and leadership coach.

My burning desire was then and is now to help all women, especially high-achieving women, build a foundation of serenity to live a thriving life. Also in 2010, I began hosting women's retreats. Retreats are my passion. I love seeing women turn the world off for a couple of days, make real connections with other women and soak up what the Holy Spirit has for them. It truly is a beautiful thing.

I began working on this book approximately four years ago. Honestly, I can't remember exactly when and I would really like to forget because I began the book, put it down, began again, put it down, and continued this cycle for a long time. But the calling for me to write this book never left me. I knew with every passing week, month, and year that I needed to make my writing a priority. I simply didn't. Fear of putting myself out to the world plagued me. And I allowed many other things to get in the way. Some of those things I can attribute to my character defects, one being the tendency to take on too much – because I can – to the detriment of other priorities. Hence, the need for this book!

Being a high-achieving woman is wonderful in so many ways, but it is also not easy. We tend to fight great battles within ourselves, trying to live up to our own expectations, and thus we create a stressful, overloaded life. Add to that, when others try to live up to our expectations, strained relationships and even more stress results.

It took some hard lessons for me to step aside from my constant busyness and choose to address head-on what I call my inner conflicts. We all have inner conflicts, things about ourselves that need to change, because they are not healthy and they keep us from thriving. Even the positive attributes of a high-achieving woman can turn into defects or inner conflicts, which can make them difficult to see and equally difficult to deal with.

You have likely heard the reference to "cycles of insanity" where a person repeats over and over the same choices and behaviors that do not serve them well. Personally, it took me most of my life to stop the cycles of insanity created by my discontent, my independent nature, the masks I wore, and so much more. In my case, alcoholism played a role as well.

Introduction

This book is intended to help high-achieving women, whether professionals in the world of work or home-makers, stop the inner conflicts (our cycles of insanity) that keep us from living a truly thriving life. Let's be real. We've realized levels of success in our careers, families, churches, and more, but we still haven't found that key to success that removes feelings that there must be something more we need to strive for. But what is it? What keeps these inner conflicts alive? Why can't we just be fulfilled with where we are and who we are? How can we be successful, yet still struggle with so much turmoil going on inside?

This book is not intended to answer all these questions in explicit detail. Rather, my intention is to provoke your awareness of how your high-achieving character feeds the inner turmoil with which you live. Awareness is the beginning. Without that, your cycles will continue to repeat themselves. Likewise, you will continue to push aside the foundational issues that drive so much of your inability to live a free and thriving life.

I've identified nine character attributes that can create significant problems within high-achieving women. These may be part of who we are, but they do not always serve us well. Through my transparency, I hope you will see that you are not alone and that your desire to thrive can be realized. You do not have to be a slave to the battles that rage within.

In my journey of always striving for fulfillment (striving to thrive), my inner conflicts supported my turning to alcohol as a solution. Granted, alcoholism was present long before, but I used alcohol as a means to escape the pressurized environment I had created. As of this writing, I am so grateful to have 12 years of sobriety. My journey in recovery is one of the best things that ever happened to me. It brought great clarity to my innate character and revealed to me how that character can bless me and curse me at the same time.

For many reasons, high-achieving women suffer from much inner turmoil. The character attributes noted in each chapter of this book can contribute, at least in part. Each chapter ends with ways to reflect on the topic in your own life and ways to thrive through it.

I have wasted a lot of years allowing my inner conflicts to create issues in my life and keep me internally miserable. If, in the reading of this book, just one other woman finds freedom from one internal battle, then I will be grateful. Secondly, but most importantly, I want to share the truth that God saved me from myself. If it weren't for Him never giving up on me, I would not have my sobriety and a family that is healthy and happy. I wouldn't be serving people rather than serving myself, and I certainly wouldn't have written this book.

If you, too, are a high-achieving woman, then like me, you have had great successes and some failures in life.

Introduction

Somewhere along the way, I learned to stop the constant striving for something more and to live a thriving life. I believe you can too.

No matter how similar we may seem, we are each one completely unique. My prayer is that you will find something in this book that resonates with your life, something that causes you to seek necessary changes in your inner conflicts that are not adding value to your life. Don't live any longer wearing an external happy face while struggling with inner turmoil.

One of my favorite quotes is by Eleanor Roosevelt, ""In the long run, we shape our lives, and we shape ourselves. The process never ends until we die. And the choices we make are ultimately our own responsibility."

Enjoy and be encouraged to live your thriving life!

Chapter 1
Discontentment

a battle for my soul,
a war for peace

Oh, the battle for peace! You run yourself ragged for days on end, trying to reach that place where you believe you've arrived and all will be right with your world. It's a constant push and strive, grinding it out day after day. Then one day you look around and ask why. "Why do I keep doing this?"

Constantly being on the go is something we high-achievers do extremely well because it's a part of who we are. By our very nature, we are movers and shakers. We have a natural gotta-get-it-done mentality. The going and doing isn't a bad thing in and of itself (you are going to hear that a lot in this book), but it becomes harmful when we believe it's where we will find a life that more than satisfies us – a thriving life.

Discontentment is the culprit that causes us to strive rather than thrive. It can be hard to see, because it gets disguised as *needs*. I need that higher paying job; I need a new car; I need to move to another city. Needs are real, yes, and we must take care of them. Many, however, are not true needs; they really are *wants*. When we look at our wants as needs, discontentment

Chapter 1
Discontentment

is at the core. Let me say that again, "When we look at our wants as needs, discontentment is at the core."

For high-achievers, this is a real problem. We are accustomed to things changing and bringing forth constant improvement. We lead the charge of making things better for people all around us. There is always something new and improved to be had. New and improved, however, simply for the sake of trying to please ourselves or others, or to seek some perceived level of contentment, ultimately creates more problems of discontentment.

How many new things have truly satisfied your deep inner being and gratified you for the long haul? What happened once the newness wore off?

I lived much of my life with immense discontentment and it drove me to absolute craziness. I wasn't just unhappy with this or that. I was unhappy with pretty much everything at some point in time. One day it might be the curtains in the living room and the next it would be my whole house. The following week it would be my husband and eventually my marriage.

Lots of things in this world drive this demon, but one that is at the top of the list for me is a lack of stillness, never taking the time to sit with God, with my own thoughts, and with others. Honestly, I didn't know that I needed the silence.

I was raised by strong, get-it-done women. My grandmother and my mother were extremely independent and always worked hard. A high work ethic is part of their character and it is part of mine. They also *had* to work hard. My grandmother raised four children on a waitress's income. My mother raised herself and me on a factory worker's income. Their situations and jobs required hard work. They taught me that nothing comes free and you work for everything you have. There was no entitlement mentality in my upbringing. I learned early on to keep a clean house, cook meals daily, do the laundry, buy the groceries, and raise my children, all while holding down a full-time job. Like my grandmother and mother, I did this for many years on my own.

I am very grateful for the many things my grandmother and mother taught me. During all this activity in my life, however, I never understood (perhaps I chose not to understand) the need for down time. My world was fast-paced, and I ate it up. I entered the corporate world at a young age, right out of high school. I remember my first year well. I hired on as an operator with the phone company in August. That same year, I spent the holidays working. I found myself resentful, however, because my family and friends were out celebrating and I was stuck working.

Little did I realize that discontentment, which hadn't even begun to fully establish itself within me yet, would be the reason I stayed at my job through those painful first holidays.   It's true that getting my first real job out of high school for a large corporation was wonderful. I would have been crazy to turn it down, and I've been thankful over and over that I didn't walk away from it. Let me just say that there was more going on than I knew at the time. God had a plan, but I didn't find that out until 30 years later (this will be revisited in the conclusion). I can also look back and see the seeds of discontentment that were forming in my soul. Eventually, I began to feel like I worked harder than my husband, that I had to care for the kids even while working full-time, that all the weight was on my shoulders. and so much more. Truly, discontentment took hold deep within me.

I have wasted lots of money, time, and energy trying to combat this demon that masquerades itself as a need. How about you? How many new pair of shoes have you purchased because they were *needed* when many pairs already existed in the closet? How many opportunities to spend time with family or friends have been lost because you *needed* to do this or that? How many times have you let go of taking care of your health because you *needed* to work? Clearly, this questioning could go on for a long time. I hope you will pause and ask yourself how many, if any, of these questions relate to your life. What other questions might you need to consider?

In 1 Corinthians 10:13, God says He will not give us more than we can handle. I fully believe that now. Unfortunately, I did not believe it during those child-rearing, corporate years when I so desperately needed to.

I had allowed discontentment to steal away what I valued most (or said I did). I spent too many years with my priorities messed up, with discontentment at the root. I finally held up the white flag of surrender and yielded to a healthy and helpful understanding that *everything I think I need is not a need and everything I want is not necessary*. This is especially true when it comes to where I spend my time. I try to no longer spend time on things that aren't adding value to my life or the lives of others or to that which is causing me to stray from the path God has for my life. There's no question that when we are living a full life of career, raising our families, and being active in our communities, it can be hard to stop and assess what is truly value-added. There's barely time to stop and think most days.

Always a Season

If there is one thing I wish I had known when my life was in full swing (there is definitely more than one thing I wish I had known!), it would be that there are seasons of life, and that no matter the season, time to simply rest is required. Resting can look different based on the season, but it has a component that never changes, and that's stopping long enough to listen for and hear the voice of God. And when it seems like God isn't speaking, it doesn't mean He wants us to step in and just do what we think makes the most sense to satisfy our souls. It means to wait and rest until we do hear His voice.

In the chaotic years of working and raising a family, resting doesn't mean that dreams or goals are forgotten; it simply means that we need to be prayerfully aware that growth is always occurring. This is true even when resting means to be content with where I am for that season, aware that I don't always have to be off on some new project or venture. Oh, the time I have wasted beginning new things (that seemed like awesome ideas) that had to be done right then. Of course, every one of those new projects was supposed to bring me some level of contentment. I did gain satisfaction for a while, but too often it never lasted.

Life is a never-ending learning process full of adventures. It's not about *arriving*. I sure wish I had understood that when I was much younger! I was always striving to arrive. What I found is that *my striving was killing me and arriving is a farce.*

When I was in the corporate world, I focused on excellence in my job and making more money. Always a person of high inner work standards, excellence for me equaled a pay raise, but it also equaled recognition. I wanted both. The greater of the two was certainly the money. If I could make more money, we could go on vacation, buy a newer car, have more clothes, and the list went on. If we went on vacation, I could get a break and life would be good. If I had a newer car and new clothes, that would certainly make things better. There was always something more that was needed to bring happiness or at least some level of satisfaction. I was always on a mission to reach a "better" life. Wanting a better life isn't a bad thing, but when the betterment is at the expense of what's truly important, discontentment will prevail.

The world is moving so fast these days. I look around and wonder how in the world people do it all. Some of my family and friends will laugh at that statement; they've said the same thing about me once or twice. I am one who will always have multiple irons in the fire. I love being involved. I am a helper and I love new projects.

The problem for me was that I allowed these positive attributes to become a bit of a curse. I used it all to believe that I should constantly be achieving something more. Achievements are great, but when the achieving comes at the expense of our relationship with God, our relationships with others, and caring for ourselves, it's a problem.

Chapter 1
Discontentment

I've learned that stillness is my best friend. Taking time to stop and listen before moving forward is the best cure for discontent that I know. When I take the time to stop and pray, I can assess what is true and what isn't. This is important, because so often the "fix" we go after to solve our discontentment is based on emotional responses, emotions fueled by those wants we disguise as needs.

In my mind, I can find the logic for needing a new car when the one I am driving is only two years old. But is it a want or a need? I am in no way suggesting that if you have the means to buy a new car every year or two, and that is what you do because you believe it's best, no problem. Please don't think I am suggesting there is something wrong with that. The issue I want to make clear is this: If we are seeking a solution to happiness or a fix for emotional ups and downs in new houses, new cars, or new husbands, that will never provide what we need.

When I take the time to be still, I can come out from under the lies of "unfairness" and "I deserve" comments that float around in my head. When I take the time to be still, I give myself the necessary margin to make decisions based on facts and a proper perspective. When I take the time to be still, I may discover that I'm not supposed to come to the rescue of everyone or fix every problem around me.

This is the same for the discontentment that drives a constant need to achieve. Do I really need to strive for that next promotion (which may or may not come) at this season of my life? When driven by discontentment, I believe I must do it and I have to do it now, that I can't wait or I'll miss the opportunity.

The question, "Is this really all there is?" rings so loudly in my mind that it becomes deafening. There's no consideration of true priorities, because the drive to achieve becomes overwhelming. Being an independent, high-achieving woman makes it hard to step back and consider that the timing may not be right. Perhaps I can't see that God may not want me to take this promotion because He has a better path for me to take. It's much easier to assume it should be done now and I am the one who must make it happen. Waiting on God is not something I want to do when I am driven by escalated emotions, because I believe my ability to thrive will be found in my achievement.

I can't remember exactly when it was that my eyes were opened to discontentment running rampant within me, so often controlling me, but I remember that when it happened, I began immediately praying against it. I prayed to be a contented person. I prayed to see the difference between wanting something and needing something. I prayed to see things with a true and proper perspective. I was tired of wasting time, money, relationships, and more because I didn't feel happy, complete, or fulfilled.

I love the freedom that a heart of contentment brings in relationships. It allows the acceptance of who and where people are. It eliminates the anxiety and drama that naturally occur when we want people to do or say what we think they should. In my case, it helps me see, and stop, my natural tendency to control others. I can own only my part in the relationship and I can leave the other person owning theirs. In this, my heart can be at peace.

I love the truth of being content with what I have and where I am. The truth of contentment reminds me that I don't need a new this or that right now. This truth keeps me aware that contentment doesn't mean an end to reaching greater heights. In fact, it gives me the freedom to know that when I am in the lane of achievement it's because that's where I'm supposed to be.

Finally, Contentment

I retired in 2008 and never dreamed that just a few months later I would be heading down an entirely new path that did not include my ideal images of retirement. I am thankful for the transformation in me that has occurred, because I can be content in not knowing exactly where this path is going to take me. This is a BIG deal for me! No high-achieving woman walks this path easily. Were it not for times of stillness that brought awareness from God, being content in not seeing what's ahead would never be acceptable.

I am a planner and I like to have the entire journey laid out before me step by step. Stepping out in faith and being content with whatever God places in front of me should be going completely against my grain. I won't lie; there are times I get a bit anxious because I can't see every step along the way before I take it. Having said this, I also firmly believe that it is because of the gift of contentment that I am able to settle down, be still, and know that it is perfectly okay that I can't see every step. I can be content in knowing I am on a path of purpose, an impact in this world I was created for. Is this true every single day? More days than not. But I do have to stay aware.

I can't lose sight of my need to be still and sit in silence with God because I can still find myself restless. I can become discontented when things aren't happening at the pace I believe they should. This is why being able to step back, see truth, and be still is so important.

After everything that's been said, I want to address a question you may have. "Is discontentment ever okay?" Of course, it is. Discontentment can be wisdom

Chapter 1
Discontentment

at work in your soul. It can be telling you something's not right. Discontentment becomes an issue when it drives a constant desire for something more or something different. When it starts owning your choices that result in unhealthy behaviors, then discontentment has become a problem that needs to be seen for what it is. If not properly recognized and dealt with, discontentment can ruin your life.

When you find yourself in a place of continually being unsettled and with thoughts like, "There's gotta be more," ask yourself what you are discontented with. What is the "it" in your life creating the emotional turmoil? Step back and assess things. Take a hard look at what you value most. More than likely, you will find that you are on a path that is not in alignment with your core values. This may or may not be something you can easily gauge on your own. It is a wise choice to get help if you need it. Either way, once you determine what is out of alignment, you will need to determine what to do about it. Doing nothing is a choice, but it is a choice that will keep discontentment alive and well.

~

"If we are seeking a solution to happiness or a fix for emotional ups and downs in new houses, new cars, or new husbands, that will never provide what we need."

Awareness is Key

Identify Your Inner Conflicts of
DISCONTENTMENT

> ❖ Where do you see discontentment at work in your life?

> ❖ How would you define the "war for peace" inside you?

> ❖ What are you willing to do to end the discontentment that plagues you?

Choose to THRIVE!

> ❖ Know the faces of discontentment:

> ❖ wants versus needs,

> ❖ selfish choices,

> ❖ broken relationships,

> ❖ the inability to be still.

> ❖ Pray for a heart of contentment.

> ❖ Assess what is true before making decisions, especially in highly emotional times.

Chapter 1
Discontentment

❖ Know your core values, revisit them often, and then make choices that keep you in alignment with what you value most.

Chapter 2
Independence

hard to tame,
hard on relationships

"I can do it!" I realize this sounds like what a 3-year-old would say, but I also realize that often I have been just like a small child, because I have said the exact same thing more times than I can possibly count. I don't always say it out loud or to anyone in particular. Most often I say it to myself, driven by thoughts like:

- It's *easier* if I just do it myself.

- I don't want to *inconvenience* or *bother* anyone.

- I'm *supposed* to do things on my own.

Let's look at these common thoughts one at a time. "It's *easier* if I just do it myself." Sometimes this may be true depending on the task at hand. For example, if I want someone to come in and pick up a task they know very little about and may never do again, sure, it probably makes more sense to just take care of it myself. In my analysis, however, this isn't typically the situation when this thought is bombarding my mind. It's much more likely the thought is being driven by some form of false superiority thinking, something like, "Why take the time

21

to show them; they won't do it right anyway." Seriously? Or it may be that I believe I can't afford the time it would take to show someone else how to complete the task. Sad.

"I don't want to *inconvenience* or *bother* anyone." And why would that be? For sure, there have been times when this is a genuine heartfelt motive, because I know the other person is going through tough times of their own. Sometimes, however, I think this is just an excuse rooted in a life-long belief that I don't need anyone's help. I may not want to see or admit that and so I fool myself into believing my motives are more about the other person. But I wonder.

"I'm *supposed* to do things on my own." Aha! Now we are getting to the real root of why our independent nature can become something that works against us. We hear it all around us that women are tough, strong, and fully capable. True, but does that mean we are supposed to take care of everything on our own?

Being an independent woman is a great character trait to have if it doesn't become an underlying badge of honor that intimidates, steals serenity, damages relationships, and has us believing we can handle life all on our own.

Not meant to do it alone

For me, allowing people to help and support me was often misunderstood. Deep down, I probably saw it as personal weakness, but honestly, I wasn't aware of my inner self enough to even recognize that, in my independent ways, I often operated from a place of shutting people out. On the surface (which is where I lived for far too many years), I simply thought I wasn't supposed to lean on anyone, and the only person I could count on was myself. In this kind of thinking, relationships suffer.

The thoughts that drive independent behaviors can be extremely self-serving. This whole "I am woman" stuff is tough for those of us who already have a rely-only-on-self nature. The mindset that says "I can do it" must be examined to ensure it serves us and others in a healthy way, rather than draining life from ourselves and others.

There have been countless times I disappointed myself and absolutely wore myself out because of my independent, gotta-do-it-all beliefs. For as long as I can remember, I have felt I was on my own. I mentioned before that I was raised by strong women who had to depend highly on themselves. The characteristics that come with the mindset of "just take care of it" were instilled in me at a young age. This isn't a bad thing until it becomes its own thing.

Chapter 2
Independence

High-achieving women who are professionals are strong in lots of ways. We work all day, come home to cook dinner, help the kids with homework, give the kids a bath, pick up toys, do a load of wash, finalize the presentation for tomorrow, all while consoling a hurting friend on the phone. Then we get up the next morning and do it all over again…and again…and again. It's no wonder the mindset of "I have to handle it all!" is so prevailing.

With five children, you can imagine that I have thrown a party or two at my home. Why do you care? Well, you probably don't. The reason I mention it is because my hospitality memories are just one place I can share with you how my independent "I have to handle it" nature could suck life from me and others. I have always been a person who likes to entertain. I also like to make all the food and have my house in "perfect" (don't ya know it had to be perfect!) shape when my guests arrive. My poor family went through living hell during these times. It occurs to me that I've never asked them, but I wonder if they wanted to run and hide when they heard we were having people over. They had to know there would be no fun involved because Sergeant Mom would be on the scene.

I gave everyone jobs to do, but I would end up going back and doing many of them over because I wanted things done a certain way. I would be a crazy person with multiple items cooking, yelling at people to do stuff, coming right behind them and doing the same "stuff," and often ending up in tears because I was stressed out of my mind.

Why couldn't I see that it was okay to let guests bring a dish if they wanted to? Why couldn't I just go with the cleaning job my husband or kids did? Why did I have to yell? Why did I always think my hands had to be in everything? It was perfectionism at its finest (destroying what should be good.) We'll deal with perfectionism in Chapter 9 (I know you can't wait for that!).

Before we continue, I have to say that I was extremely thankful when I became aware that I wasn't exercising hospitality in all my craziness, that hospitality isn't about everything being perfect. It's about enjoying my guests. I couldn't enjoy them because I was too worried about how my house looked, if the kids were dressed properly, and if the food was staying filled and hot. I missed out on the most important part. I still love to host gatherings, but it looks very different than it did in those days. Thankfully!

My belief that I had to rely on myself kept me from reaching out to embrace the love of others when I really needed people. When using alcohol to relieve my stress became a road of self-destruction, I believed I had to handle that, too, on my own. I never let anyone get to close because I was afraid of what they would think; I didn't want to hear what they would say and I'm

Chapter 2
Independence

sure I thought I knew better. Furthermore, I believed that I had gotten myself into the messes I found myself in, so it clearly had to be for me to get myself out of them. Why would I bother anyone else for advice or direction?

Both sides of the independence coin

Relationships are hard when we lavish in our independence. Secrets are easy to keep and distance seems like a good thing. Sadly, a woman who believes this will never be fulfilled, because no person is made for total independence. We are made for relationship. The further we go in the opposite direction, the more our belief in independence grows, the more we believe the lie that it's a good thing, and the unhappier we become.

Independence, like anything else, isn't a bad thing in and of itself. The problem is when independence isolates us and creates unhealthy behaviors. On the other side of the coin, independence fosters many great things. I know several women who lack an independent nature, and they struggle with so much in their lives. We who have a natural tendency towards independence can help other women grow in self-confidence, strength, and courage.

Staying aware of our independent nature is required to have meaningful relationships.   We may have to get over ourselves and our ill-founded beliefs:

- that we don't need others

- that doing things on our own is better

- that not wanting to "bother" people is a good thing

- that we have no one we can lean on

The culprits of an independent nature that sabotage relationships come in many disguises.   Subconsciously, it can be a form of self-protection, like becoming non-communicative and retreating into ourselves. We women are all too good at this! How many times have I expected my husband to pick up on my mood and know exactly what I was thinking? Minimally, he should know that he's supposed to ask me what's wrong, right? Why would I put up a disguise instead of just sharing my feelings that I was angry or hurt? Because that would require me to be vulnerable, and vulnerability nearly always includes a huge element of fear. Fear then raises the need to protect ourselves. The need to protect ourselves fosters the ugly side of independence that says, "I can do it on my own." A vicious cycle ensues.

Chapter 2
Independence

The same thing can happen with friends or colleagues. I would have no problem putting you in the time-out corner of my world if I felt it was warranted. After all, I was going to protect my feelings and myself from the pain of whatever I believed was going on. Sadly, this type of thinking only brings more pain and helps no one.

Finding truth during our life situations is a must. Relationships are critical and required. We will never have real peace if we stay in the belief that going through life as independently as possible is a good thing.

I am thankful to understand that my independence is a good thing, but that it can also be damaging. Because independence is at the very core of who we are as high-achievers, we must stay aware and keep an eye on it. It is so easy to fall into a place where our independence does not serve us well.

I still have times when I hear the voice in my head saying the same old lies. When I do, I have a choice. I can take hold of those thoughts and call them lies or I can fall into the trap of believing them. If you and I do not stay keenly aware, operating in our independence can cause others to feel inferior and not needed. We can come across as quite intimidating. This makes frequent self-assessment critical. I know there have been times when I intimidated others when I had no intention to so.

The constant need to be on the move and conquer what is in front of us makes relationship-building difficult. It's not a conscious thought to just pass people by, but it happens all the time. It takes effort to slow down and focus on the relationships, rather than to steamroll people. It takes a huge effort to step out of our independent nature to ensure that others know they are valued more than the task(s) at hand. Nurturing people makes them feel valued, but it is not easily exercised in the hectic world of high-achieving women.

Don't assume that people know you care. Most have heard the quote by Theodore Roosevelt, "No one cares how much you know, until they know how much you care."

As a high-achieving woman, you are a natural leader and your independent nature is clearly a great asset. When you focus on showing others how important they are, and how much you care, the result will be strong relationships that speak volumes in your personal and professional fulfillment.

~

"Relationships are hard when we lavish in our independence. Secrets are easy to keep and distance seems like a good thing."

Chapter 2
Independence

Awareness is Key

Identify Your Inner Conflicts of INDEPENDENCE

- ❖ How has your independence been hard to manage?

- ❖ How has independence affected your relationships?

- ❖ If you could change one thing about your independent nature, what would it be?

Choose to THRIVE!

- ❖ Stay aware of relationship-building in your very busy life.

- ❖ Have a plan for nurturing relationships.

- ❖ Pray for a willingness to step out of your independent nature to put others first.

- ❖ Stay in a place of thankfulness for your family, friends, and co-workers.

Chapter 3
Insecurities

has many sources,
plagues all women

The words *insecurity*, *self-doubt*, and *high-achieving woman* seem like an oxymoron to me, at least on the surface. I mean, seriously, I am WOMAN, right? I can keep any number of balls in the air all at once with relative ease. So, what's up with the pit that often resides deep inside my gut?

When I think about some facts of my life, yet the pit remains, I am bewildered. Facts like:

- I birthed four children, two of them natural

- I am step-mom to one

- I am grandma (aka "maw-maw") to ten (presently) and great maw-maw to one

- I managed the integration/growth/outsourcing/insourcing of critical corporate teams

- I started my own business; twice

- I went through a divorce and later remarried

Chapter 3
Insecurities

- I participated in the leadership efforts to start a new ministry; as a very new Christian

- I survived hysterectomy-induced menopause

These are just a few of the highlights and most went on simultaneously. So, what in the world is up with any level of insecurity and self-doubt being able to survive within me! Your list of "highlights" may be even longer and you wonder the same thing.

As I have pondered the question of "Where in the world does this insecurity come from?" I have become aware of several culprits that feed my feelings of self-doubt. One is the truth that I am my own worst enemy. Self-criticism, no matter how successful I was or may be, pretty much had its way with me because I constantly compared myself to others.

For years, I thought I saw in other women what I felt I wanted or was supposed to be. I want to share a story that I hope you will find some humor in, but also, I hope you can replace the details with those that would best fit for you.

I remember a wonderful lady I once worked with. She appeared to have the perfect family; she always seemed to be on top of her game; she dressed for success; and she wore the most beautiful jewelry. Not just any jewelry, but expensive diamond jewelry. Now I have been a jewelry lover all my life. I get it honestly from my grandmother. She always wore multiple necklaces and rings. In fact, she had many necklaces with earrings and bracelets to match. I loved, loved, loved getting to play in her jewelry box when I was a child. I still have much of her jewelry and now my granddaughters get the privilege of playing with it.

If you asked my husband today, he would undoubtedly tell you that I own way too much jewelry. On second thought, let's just not ask him that question! He would be correct though. I do own way more than any one person can wear. But I digress. Back to my jewelry lady story...

I watched this lady who had this beautiful jewelry and I was envious. I was insecure about my couple of small diamond pieces and I wanted what she had. There were a couple of times the envy drove me over the edge and I spent money we didn't have on jewelry I didn't need. Materialism run amuck! Did that jealously and desire for things I didn't need cure my insecurities? Of course, not.

This woman seemed so sure of herself. Honestly, I thought if I could lose some weight (she was the "perfect" size, of course) and wear some really nice clothes and jewelry like she did then I would be the self-confident woman everybody thought I was. Seriously?

Chapter 3
Insecurities

The comparison trap that women fall into is destructive. It deepens existing insecurities and breeds new ones. Comparing myself to another woman and wanting what I think I "see" is an age-old problem for me. I know I'm not alone. We impose upon ourselves the pain of feeling "less than" if we can't do or have what we think we see in others.

Somebody else will always appear to have a better marriage, more friends, the perfect personality, more money. Someone else will always seem smarter, wiser, more courageous, more connected. We all have little seeds residing deep within us that get fertilized by the desire for something we believe others have that we don't have.

I know we all have countless stories of falling into this trap. Unfortunately, we have lots of help that drives us to it. Television and social media are not our friends in this regard. They can keep the cycle of insanity alive and well: envy, compare, beat up self and repeat.

Running from the real me

I have never known my biological father. While I've never been through counseling about this, I am sure I would be told that this is the source of much insecurity and many poor choices I have made in my life. And there may be some truth in that, but it really isn't the point I want to focus on.

What I have discovered on my journey is that the real source of my insecurities and self-doubts was in not knowing myself and seeming to live on a mission to run from the real me. I escaped focusing on who I was through many avenues. The more I compared myself to others, the more I tried to be someone I thought I was supposed to be. The more I couldn't live up to who I thought I was supposed to be, the more I criticized myself and the more I looked for ways to escape. The more I looked for ways to escape, the more discouraged I became about life.

When I got serious about my walk with Jesus and about my recovery, I stopped running and began considering "Who am I, really?" I remember working through *The Purpose Driven Life* by Rick Warren. (Warren 2012) In the first few pages of his book, he writes, "No one is a mistake." Reading that sentence had a big impact on me. I began to understand and truly believe that I was created by design and with real purpose. This truth helped me "be okay" with getting to know the real me and understanding what makes me who I am. With this knowledge, over time, all those insecurities pretty much disappeared and the pit in my stomach disintegrated. This didn't happen overnight; getting to know the real me has been a journey and still

Chapter 3
Insecurities

is. I've found things I like and things I didn't like about myself, and I still do.

One thing I found is that I am not a constant smiler. I know people who smile all the time and I've always envied that. Somehow in my over-active comparison mind, I thought that continuously smiling was a great attribute to have. I still think it is, if it's natural. Here's the thing, trying to make myself do something that doesn't come natural, just because I think I'm supposed to or it will make people like me more, keeps me in that place of trying to be someone or something I'm not. God never said, "Thou shalt smile, smile, smile." This truth helps me understand that every single person is unique. And it's okay if I don't smile as much as another person. If smiling is something I want to do more of, great! I can work on that and it will likely become natural. Forcing it for the wrong reason is not the answer.

Smiling may sound like a somewhat silly example, but I'm sure you realize that smiling is not the point. I am who I am. God created me. That's my true source of life, and it's true for every person on the planet. In the course of living, our environments and circumstances mold us and shape us. It's easy to lose sight of who we really are underneath all the other influences.

I made a ton of assumptions about myself and my life. Getting to know myself, my Creator, and who He created me to be was something I discovered later in life. It is a necessity that I hope you have already discovered. That might seem obvious to some, but when insecurities run high, so does running from the real you.

Who God created me to be

I learned that to make peace with myself, I had to know God and I had to allow Him to help me understand who He created me to be. In that learning, I found that God wants what is best for me and that even though some things are an integral part of who I am, that doesn't mean I can't do anything about them.

Let's take alcoholism as an example. Alcoholism runs in my family. Two people that I loved very much passed away because of it: my grandfather and my uncle. Like them, I've got this disease, but that doesn't mean I have to succumb to it. That's not what God desires for me. He desires that I lean on Him for the strength, courage, and faith to win that battle. Alcoholism was also a huge culprit behind my insecurities. I used it to run from myself and everyone else, escaping to a false sense of security.

Chapter 3
Insecurities

I was plagued by lies that told me I wasn't good enough, I wasn't all I should be, I couldn't do this or that, I would never achieve the things I desired (or thought I desired), other women were perfect, and on and on. Thankfully, as I grew in my relationship with God, I began to see the person He created in me. I came to realize that buying into my self-doubt and insecurities kept me from knowing and being that person. Rather than trying to know myself and grow myself, I wasted years allowing insecurities to fuel anxiety, sadness, and trying to be someone other than the beautiful, wonderful woman God created me to be.

In alignment with the lies we believe comes the problem of limiting beliefs. A limiting belief is a lie you tell yourself. It's a lie that keeps you stuck and makes you think that where you are is good enough. Let's say you desire to lose 40 pounds. You lose 20 and are proud of yourself. You feel much better and your clothes fit better. You are excited to continue your journey and can't wait to watch the numbers on that scale keep dropping. About two weeks later, the scale hasn't moved and you realize you've plateaued.

Let's also say that you've been around this block before with weight loss, and now you factor in the reality that you are older and your metabolism just isn't the same. Maybe you give it another couple of weeks. And with no movement on the scale, you conclude that the 20 pounds is good enough. You tell yourself it would be just too hard to continue and you probably wouldn't get there anyway. You justify believing this and you've just limited yourself to what you are able to achieve. That's a limiting belief.

Many women hold themselves back because they have bought into a mindset that tells them they can't go any further. Oddly enough, this happens all the time with success possibilities. The fear of achieving the success you are on the path for drives a belief that failure is imminent. This belief causes you to hold yourself back from reaching for what you are truly capable of.

When you hear, yourself saying the words "I can't," it's time to start looking for what belief is causing you to think that way. I'm not suggesting that you live in a world with no reality, but I am suggesting that you make sure the reality is based on truth. Limiting beliefs are grounded in assumptions and fears that drive insecurities. These insecurities, in turn, limit what you believe about yourself.

For high-achieving women, there typically isn't much we won't at least try to go after. That doesn't change the fact that we, too, struggle with limiting beliefs; we just do a pretty good job at hiding that fact.

Insecurities hit everyone. They can serve a valuable purpose when the good and bad are understood. Insecurities, when used as fuel to see what is true and to spur on perseverance is a good thing. Too often insecurities take on lives of their own, and deep down we feel threatened in some way. We allow our capabilities to be stifled, we do not reach out to live our God-given life purpose, and we try to be someone other than the person God created us to be.

Not alone

For me, it was a big revelation to discover that I wasn't alone. No matter how confident other women appeared, they also struggled with insecurities. Knowing this truth helped me step out and speak up.

Serving as the ministry leader, alongside my husband, and serving women through Celebrate Recovery has been an awesome journey. (For more information, visit: http://celebraterecovery.com). Women, and men, from all walks of life come to find healing from the insecurities that plague them. I have been grateful to have been given the first-hand experience of working with women in corporate settings and women who are far removed from that type of environment. The truth is, we aren't so different when it comes down to our innermost being. Circumstances are certainly different, but our internal struggles are quite similar.

We want to be secure in who we are and we want to be secure in what we are here to do while on this earth. We want to value ourselves and to be valued by others. We want to walk firmly and give back generously. We want to love and be loved.

It saddens me to recall the many years I allowed my insecurities to hold me back in one way or another, as well as the many poor choices I've made attempting to fill the voids created by allowing those insecurities to run rampant within me. I have had to step back and look at what is true. For instance, when I am about speak in front of an audience, I still have nervous energy and hear a voice that says, "Who do you think you are?" or "You're going to look like a fool." I must remember what is true. I am coming in front of this group by design. I'm not there by chance!

I use affirmations that remind me of this and the fact that I have things to say that will help other people. I am reminded that God has called me to share my story and it's His job to determine who will hear it and what they will do with what they hear.

I share parts of my story often because being able to talk about it, especially the insecurities, is huge. Not only does this help me remember how far I've come, but also there is always something there that helps someone else. As long as I hold my struggles in, how-

Chapter 3
Insecurities

ever, they can become an entity of their own and neg-
atively impact my thoughts and emotions. I have discovered that I find true serenity in removing the power
of my insecurities by keeping them out in the open.

~

*"Insecurities hit everyone. They can serve a valuable
purpose when the good and bad are understood."*

Awareness is Key

Identify Your Inner Conflicts of INSECURITIES

❖ How have insecurities plagued you?

❖ How have you been able to disarm your insecurities?

❖ What problems have your insecurities created for your loved ones?

Choose to THRIVE!

❖ Get to know the deepest part of who God created you to be.

❖ Seek out a spiritual mentor.

❖ Be aware of things like the comparison trap and beliefs that simply don't serve to add value.

❖ Share your insecurities. Don't give them any power by keeping them hidden

Chapter 4
Loneliness

so very painful,
so unnecessary

It would seem, all women struggle at times with feelings of loneliness. I have lived with those feelings for most of my life. As an only child of a single working mother, I naturally had times where I was physically alone. Too much alone time as a child was not a good thing. As an adult, though, being physically alone is not what drives the emotional loneliness that can be so hard to overcome. Like many, I enjoy my times of being physically alone. No phones ringing, people talking, TV blaring, or other noises. A little solitude is a beautiful thing!

For high-achieving women, finding times for physical solitude are hard to come by; times of emotional loneliness, however, are not. We naturally gravitate to leadership roles, where there are lots of situations and circumstances that include emotional loneliness. It comes with the territory. Leaders will always find themselves holding information that must be kept confidential, where you can't talk about things with most people. So, you are left alone with your thoughts. This, in and of itself, isn't an issue. It comes with being in those positions where confidentiality is required. The problem is when this is coupled with so many other life situations that foster feelings of loneliness.

Who will listen to me?

In my life, I seemed to always be the one with a sign on my head that read, "Tell me your problems." This, too, comes with the territory of being a high-achieving woman. People naturally see you as someone who can shoulder their pain; and you likely have some helpful advice for them. The problem for me was that I needed people I could go to, but I never felt like I had anyone because they were all coming to me.

Family, friends, colleagues, and employees would tell me their problems. Sometimes they just wanted me to listen and sometimes they were looking for guidance and advice. No doubt this has contributed to my deep passion for wanting to help others. I wouldn't trade this part of my life for anything. And it's ongoing to this day. I do have broad shoulders and that is by divine design. Even so, when I think about the times when I felt so all alone, I can see now how people always coming to me was a contributing factor to my loneliness.

You see, when others came to me with their problems, in confidence, it left me alone with my thoughts – and theirs. Multiply this by some factor given the season of life. What I mean is this, when one person comes to tell you their problems, there will inevitably be two or three more who will do the same thing. It seems to come in seasons where multiple people all at the same time are looking for confidential help and guidance.

Consider my role as confidential listener and guide to others, when at the same time throughout those years I was hiding my own dysfunctional behaviors. The emotional loneliness became overpowering. Add my high-achieving nature and it gets even more difficult.

I've always carried high expectations of myself and others. When I or others don't perform, or produce equal to what I expect, I end up feeling alone again. The thoughts of disappointment, questions of "Am I expecting too much?" and wonderings of where to go from here play over and over in my mind. Could I discuss this with someone? Sure! If I weren't this highly proclaimed, self-sufficient professional, high-achieving woman who believes I should handle everything on my own. But I did believe that.

So, I would keep it all to myself and wallow in my thoughts, allowing feelings of being in it alone, yet again, creep in and take over my mind. It's a vicious cycle of believing I can't count on anyone, including myself, and that leads to not wanting to have anything to do with other people. That people continually came to me for help in my dysfunctional days is an interesting paradox, because I couldn't seem to help myself.

Another interesting paradox related to loneliness is feeling alone in a crowd. I have often experienced walking into an event, gathering, or meeting and feeling completely out of place. The committee in my head starts speaking loudly, telling me I don't fit in, I'm dressed wrong, and all sorts of other self-defeating thoughts. When I bought into this junk, I began to immediately shut people out. I can start engaging in the conversation of lies filling my head, and then low self-esteem kicks into overdrive. Feelings of worthlessness run amuck. Absolute garbage was allowed to take on a life of its own.

No doubt some of this was driven by not feeling like one of the crowd, one of the insiders. I have almost never been an "insider," because I have never played the games well that many play. Professionally, I was on the outside of many peer groups simply because I lost patience for the worthless activities of gossip, lack of authenticity, self-serving, one-sided conversations, and what seemed to be pointless discussions. Interestingly, this is key to what I came to learn about myself.

One of my core values is excellence. I enjoy doing things with a level of excellence and I desire that from others. Things like superficial conversations do not fit my idea of excellence. Conversations where someone gives no consideration to relevancy or wise use of my time do not fit my idea of excellence. The problem here is that I lost sight of the need to allow people their own space in their own way. I tried to fit people into my mold of how they should express themselves instead of letting them be who they are. At the root, I discovered that I had lost sight of heartfelt compassion. Feeling like an outsider had cost me the art of conversation and the value of relationships. People need to express themselves and everyone does that differently.

It's all about connecting

In my career, I was also on the outside of friend and colleague groups because I was frequently off to conquer some task or project. Would the work have been there when I returned? You bet it would. Did the 45-60 minutes it would have taken to have lunch with others make or break the project? Almost never.

The definition of loneliness says that it's sadness because one has no friends or company. Thus, it's about not feeling connected to people. It's a lack of relationship. You can be in the middle of many people and not be connecting.

One of the John C. Maxwell programs that I teach and speak on is called "Everyone Communicates, Few

Connect." This is one of my favorites because connection is vital to our existence, and deep connection for high-achieving women is so tough. As leaders, we have lots of so-called friends, but we have to ask ourselves how deep do those relationships really go? My experience is that most do not run very deep.

I have attended many events where I would put on my happy face, but could have cared less about connecting with anyone. Business events were often filled with superficial conversations where no one was interested in a real connection because of the competitive environment. Many that appeared to be interested in connecting were doing it because they wanted something from me, a promotion, the next big project, an inside scoop, you name it. I've had the same feelings at many non-business events as well.

The underlying problem in all of this was not others, but me. I wasn't very wise in my younger years, and so judging the motives of others kept me assuming I had to have my guard up constantly. This, in turn, kept me from seeking authentic connections. I can honestly say that I have never been in a crowd where I couldn't connect with someone if I had wanted to. Loneliness is a choice.

"Sadness because one has no friends." As I ponder this part of the definition of loneliness, I think about many supposed friends I have had over my life. Many of them have not really been friends at all. They have been acquaintances, but not people that I could call upon in a crisis or share my deepest struggles. I am thankful for them; it's just necessary for me to be real about who they are in my life. Recognizing the difference allows me to put expectations in their proper place and hopefully avoid hurt feelings. The relationships we have on social media make this another paradox. I don't know about you, but I have tons of Facebook "friends" that I don't really know.

I have had few close friends in my life. I am grateful to have more today than ever before.

Being older and seeing the world through a different set of lens has its advantages. During my younger years of high dysfunction, not having close friends was my doing. I had people who would have been there for me, but I wouldn't let them in. Secrets and believing I had to figure things out on my own drove me to erect perceived barriers of self-protection. In turn, those barriers drove isolation. Isolation always drives emotional loneliness. The more we isolate, the more we die on the inside.

Chapter 4
Loneliness

Hopelessness, right around the corner

I remember struggling with this chapter. One evening, as I was attempting to write, I could hardly get past the first couple of sentences. The words were just not coming. Finally, I put it down, thinking I'd give it a little while and come back to it later. This was about 7:30 p. m. Next thing I knew, I found myself barely able to stay awake. At the time, I remember trying to figure out why I was so tired since I had slept well the night before and wasn't at all tired during the day. I kept dosing off and on until about 9:15, when I finally gave up and went to bed.

The next day for me was a full calendar of events, but I knew I wanted to work on this chapter, so I set my alarm for 4:15 a.m. I wanted to have my devotional and prayer time, go to the gym, and still get a little time in on my writing before heading out for the day. When I set my alarm the night before, I remembered thinking, how in the world am I going to get up that early? I am an early riser, but 4:15 a.m. is a push!

The next morning I surprised myself when I had no problem getting up when the alarm went off. As always, coffee in hand, I opened my Bible app to continue reading my daily devotional plan. I was taken to Mark 15 and I quickly realized this was no coincidence. This chapter in the Gospel of Mark shares Jesus' crucifixion. Jesus was completely alone in what He had to do. He even asked God "why" when He was on the cross. Psalm 22:1 (NLT) states: "My God, My God, why have you abandoned me?" Nothing in my life, or yours, could ever compare to the level of loneliness Jesus lived through that day. God used this reading to move my heart and lift the mental block I had about writing this chapter.

I remember many times losing hope as the disease of alcoholism progressed in my life. I can also remember times of losing hope at what I experienced through the behaviors of others. Those have been the loneliest times in my life journey. Thankfully, much time has passed since then, but I try not to take this for granted and stay aware that that kind of hopelessness could be right around any corner.

Emotional loneliness is tough and it shouldn't be taken lightly. Women especially are prone to feeling alone and all too easily seek solutions that eventually drive us deeper into it rather than lift us out of it. Partly this is true because we don't really know what we are after. We know we want to eliminate the feelings of loneliness, but we don't step far enough back to fully consider what we are expecting. How will we know when we get there? And what situations or people in our lives are contributing factors? What needs to change?

Chapter 4
Loneliness

One of the greatest mistakes I made was to believe I was alone in dealing with my full and stressful life. Because I believed this, I sought out relief and times of escape through alcohol, infidelity, workaholism, and shopping. Every single one of these perceived solutions drove me into greater loneliness and self-perceived abandonment.

The struggle with loneliness is no different from many other things we self-sufficient, high-achieving women have to learn the truth about. First, the struggle of loneliness is inherent in our nature. The fact is that we naturally lead, people share their secrets with us, and we depend so highly on ourselves. Because these characteristics are true, it is imperative that we keep ourselves engaged in positive ways to not let the burden of loneliness overtake us. Secondly, we have a choice to put people and connecting with them first. We have a choice to step out of our overwhelming need to protect ourselves.

Now when loneliness tries to burden me, I take a step back and look at what is true. The truth being: I am never alone unless I choose to be. I still operate in multiple leadership roles where people continually come to me for help and seek my confidence. That's a beautiful thing in who God made me to be! And I love it. Just like anything else, what was made for good can be used against me if I do not stay aware and in authentic truth.

I'm older and I've picked up some wisdom along the path. Not much has changed in the world we live in. A lot has changed inside me, though, including how I choose to see the world.

~

"Isolation always drives emotional loneliness. The more we isolate, the more we die inside."

Chapter 4
Loneliness

Awareness is Key

Identify Your Inner Conflicts of LONELINESS

- ❖ Has loneliness been an issue for you? How so?

- ❖ Do you believe loneliness is a choice? Why or why not?

- ❖ What are the affects you have seen from isolating yourself?

Choose to THRIVE!

- ❖ Draw closer to the true friends you have, or set out to make new true friends.

- ❖ Focus on adding value to others and relationship-building.

- ❖ When feeling lonely in a crowd, step out of your comfort zone to engage with others.

- ❖ Go deeper than communication by seeking connection.

Chapter 5
Masks

feeling like an imposter,
wondering who I really am

"Will the real me please stand up!" I ran from myself for so long that the only thing I knew about me, it seems, was my name. Okay, so that's not quite true. I guess I knew my favorite color as well, because I can't remember ever having another other than blue. But besides that, I really didn't know much about who I was. One, I was lost in the world of being all things to all people, and, two, I was trying to escape my stress-filled life. In fact, I spent lots of time trying to escape my stress-filled life… *lots* of time.

Just couldn't say no

My stress came from every possible direction, but most of it was by my own doing.   Let's take my career, for example. I was quite successful in my corporate days from multiple perspectives, not the least of which included my salary and recognition for a job well done. But I always had too much on my plate. I really didn't know how to say "no," nor did I want to. I always picked up the next project even though I was already stressed out just trying to keep my head above water working on my current projects. I thought it was what I had to do. After all, I wanted to make more money and I wanted to demonstrate to myself and others that I was capable. Therefore, I couldn't say "no." At least that's what my mind told me and I bought into it.

One result of not being able to say no that always bothered me was never having the time I wanted to dig more deeply into any one project, where I could feel like I knew it inside and out. I always felt like a "jack of all trades, master of none." I wanted to fully understand the things my teams worked on, but I simply couldn't. Looking back, I did not have the mental capacity for it all. Some would say that as a leader I didn't need to know all the details. I get that, and I can agree on some level. But I never liked it. It created a ton of stress for me because I felt like an imposter when I had to represent projects but didn't have all the knowledge I wanted or felt I should have. This was just one of the ways I felt like an imposter in my workplace.

In another area, although I had friends at work that I love dearly to this day, I wore my corporate hat believing I had to be careful with how close I let anyone get. I suppose in some ways it's the nature of the beast, but I struggled with being the manager/supervisor and feeling a lack of genuine closeness to those with whom I worked. Friendships held a level of needing to stay professional, which meant there were many things I couldn't discuss or conversations I needed to temper. Even with friends in my peer group, there were always "off limit" items, personally and professionally.

In my family, I attempted to be supermom, wearing the hat, the cape, tights, and, oh yes, the mask. I can remember insisting that my children have a hot, home-cooked meal every day before they went to school (okay, for my younger children reading this, this was the first two kids). I worked in an office 50 miles away from home, but I carried a lot of guilt if they didn't have that hot meal. I wouldn't tell my children they couldn't be involved in activities so I pushed myself to try and keep my job from getting in the way of that. I was a single mom (even when married) for many of these years, which made me push even harder. The expectations I placed on myself were substantial. My mask was huge. I had to take care of it all, and felt I was on my own to do it.

At church, I wore my holy-on-Sundays mask. Gotta look like all is good, right? I found that church can be an environment filled with superficial relationships. I remember a sermon one time where my minister talked about the standard responses we give when asked, "How are you?" Most respond along the lines of, "Fine," "I'm fine," or "Doing fine." Often, I feel that the person doing the asking really doesn't care a great deal about how I'm doing. Their question is just as standard as my answer, "Just fine."

Chapter 5
Masks

I don't remember anymore what the topic of the sermon was. Perhaps something along the lines of authenticity or honesty, but, once again, my imposter awareness was heightened because I was hardly ever "fine" in those days. Being authentic wasn't something I could handle, and I'm certain I thought no else could have handled my authenticity either! Seriously, what would that look like? "How are you, Debbie?" "Oh, you know, I can't stand myself right now. How are you?"

When I came out and admitted to being a high-functioning alcoholic, I had people argue with me about it. "No, you're not!" was the response from many of them. "Oh, yes, I am," I answered. When I exposed this truth to one friend whom I hadn't seen in years, she practically yelled at me. "No, you had it all goin' on!" I proceeded to tell her that I worked hard for people to think just that. Guess it worked with some folks. Oh, the mask of deception.

Hiding behind my secrets

I got so used to keeping my secrets that being an imposter became a way of life. For high-achieving women, the pressure we place on ourselves to be perfect and strong in every way is huge. Allowing ourselves to be seen anything but totally in control just doesn't fit well with our image of who we believe we are supposed to be. Sadly, the image we assume we should have is for someone who can't exist.

Perfection is simply an illusion. The more we strive for it, the more inauthentic we become and the greater the need for the appearance that we are someone other than who we really are. And (you know where this is going), the more we feel like imposters, because, well, that's exactly what we are. Pull another mask off the shelf.

Any time secrets are alive and well, so is the imposter syndrome. Anytime we believe there is no one with whom we can share our struggles, the imposter syndrome is in high gear. I didn't realize any of this truth for many years. I thought it was simply the way life had to be for someone like myself. I honestly thought that no one else had all the same life issues I did. Therefore, I had to hide and they didn't.

Eventually, I did realize my lack of authenticity, but I continued to put on a front and hide behind my secrets. I became afraid of what life would be without the me I knew. Mind you, I had reached the point where I didn't like that me, but she was all I knew. My mother-in-law coined a phrase that I love, "artificial personality." These are people trying to be who they think they are supposed to be rather than who they were created to be. I think this phrase is right on, and its way too prevalent in the world in which we live.

Chapter 5
Masks

What is it about our genuine self that scares us? I can't count how many times I have heard these words from women I've been blessed to help: "What if no one likes the real me?" I've asked this same type of question way too many times! Think about how many dysfunctional behaviors are fueled by this one question. No wonder we put on masks and try to be someone we aren't.

Accepting the truth

In recovery programs, people must learn to know themselves and love themselves for who they are. This is not easy. I hated my struggle with alcohol, and I was mad at God and the world for a long time. How could I possibly love myself as an alcoholic? All I could see were the bad choices I had made and the person I desperately wanted to be. Knowing and loving my genuine self included the acceptance of the truth that I had no control over alcohol and that I have a disease that will be with me forever. Whether I like it or not is not the issue. Acceptance is the issue. If I chose to accept this truth, I could move forward in positive ways that develop authenticity, and I could use it to help others. If I chose to deny this truth, I would stay stuck in my bitterness and continue to hide behind my masks.

Replace alcohol in the above paragraph with a pain point about yourself that causes you to throw up the defense mechanism of putting on a mask. I'm here to tell you that our masks wear us out and wear us down. They create more and more pressure as we feel the need to portray an artificial personality.

Fact is, we all have things about ourselves that we either know needs to be different or we simply wish were different. Either way, we are faced with choices. We can be responsible for our character defects and take the high road to overcoming them or we can pretend they don't exist. When we choose to work through them, a cool outcome bursts forth: we grow and mature into truly authentic people who help others grow and mature into truly authentic people. The result is people living their God-given purpose through lives that thrive.

Taking off our masks isn't easy. So many fears spring forth as we think about others knowing who we really are, that we are flawed people. Getting beyond this fear requires giving up our concerns about what other people think. The only way I know for this to happen is to believe that we have only one Judge that we will someday meet: Jesus Christ. No one in this world has the right to judge me or you. Do people do it anyway? Yes, but you must leave that dysfunctional behavior with them. I know it's not easy, but it's worth working hard at.

Chapter 5
Masks

Getting over the worry of what other people think opened incredible doors to self-confidence. And it afforded me the ability to step out in faith to the work God was calling me to, like writing this book. Whatever God calls you to, being your authentic self will make the path much easier to walk.

~

"Any time secrets are alive and well, so is the imposter syndrome. Any time we believe there is no one we can share our struggles with, the imposter syndrome is in high gear."

Awareness is Key

Identify Your Inner Conflicts of MASKS

- ❖ What mask(s) do you wear?

- ❖ What is it about yourself that causes you to put on your mask(s)?

- ❖ What are you willing to do to eliminate your mask(s)?

Choose to THRIVE!

- ❖ Pray and ask God to take you deep within the person He created you to be.

- ❖ Journal what you hear from God and share this with a trusted friend, counselor, life coach, or pastor.

- ❖ Identify the triggers that cause you to put on the mask(s) you often wear.

- ❖ Seek accountability in replacing your mask(s) with your authentic self.

Chapter 6
Self-Sabotage

tough to admit,
tougher to change

Self-sabotage. Oh, how many ways do we harm ourselves? How many ways do we hold ourselves back from being the truly great people we were created to be? Self-sabotage comes in many forms:

- overeating

- perfectionism

- extra-marital affairs

- misusing alcohol or medications

- being a workaholic

- a lack of self-care

- constantly being on-the-go

- never being still

- and many other harmful behaviors.

Chapter 6
Self-Sabotage

No question that the busy lives of high-achieving women make it difficult to avoid self-sabotaging behaviors. There is no shortage of stress, but there always seems to be a huge shortage of time. This is the way life is and it doesn't make life easy. Turning to behaviors that do not serve us well does not have to be the status quo.

Today's world is more fast-paced than it's ever been. But that doesn't mean it has to own you and drive you to unhealthy choices. Every high-achieving woman must look at her life and determine what is truly necessary and what can be eliminated. Upon first thought, it will look like everything must be done. This, however, is likely not true. We will discuss the topic of boundaries in Chapter 10.

For now, let's take a closer look at self-sabotage by the categories of physical wellness, emotional wellness, spiritual wellness, and overall wellness:

Physical wellness suffers when we don't eat right, when we stay too busy to exercise, when we don't get proper sleep, when we abuse alcohol or other substances. I truly know the arguments for not having enough time to properly take care of your physical wellbeing. I fully understand that there are only so many hours in the day. And I know that you've heard it all before, that caring for yourself must come first. So, what could I say that will help you find a little time to take care of you?

I don't have any magic words or solutions. I can only share from my own experience. I always thought I had to figure out some way to find extra time in the day. In addition, I thought I needed an hour-plus to exercise. If I didn't have that much time, then "Why bother?" I thought. However, the saying that we've heard for more years than we can remember is true: "a little goes a long way."

I decided that I would visit the gym 3-4 days a week, and if all I could give was 20 minutes, then that was all I would give. It was hard at first because I had to fight the negative thoughts of "why bother?" I am so thankful I stuck with my plan then and still do today, because the payoff has been HUGE! My energy level stays up, my mood remains good, and my motivation has increased. I love it! If I can't make it to the gym due to weather or some other compelling reason, I can walk around my house or up and down the stairs for 15-20 minutes. The point is, I don't want to risk losing my desire for healthy movement and do nothing, which, in turn, brings unhealthy results.

The same applies to the food I eat. I would let myself get overwhelmed at the thought of cooking healthy meals before I had even given it a real shot. When my kids were young, I developed a routine of getting up

Chapter 6
Self-Sabotage

early on Saturday mornings to cook meals for the entire week. This kept me from running to the grocery store every day when I needed to get home from work and get dinner on the table. It kept me from grabbing pizza or fast food. And it helped me feed my family foods that I thought were good for us. Side trip here. In those days, I'm not so sure the food was necessarily healthy, but it was homemade.

I began taking my lunch to work, which saved money, and again I didn't run to food that would pack on the pounds I didn't need. Certainly, business lunches and travel made this a challenge. But restaurants have come a long way in offering choices that are healthy. In my corporate days, this wasn't really the case although salads were always an option. For several years, I traveled a LOT for work, which meant eating out three times a day and trying to make smart choices. I can remember making myself visit the pool in the hotels daily to swim laps, and I utilized walking trails where available. Thankfully, healthy eating is something we hear about all the time and the options are pretty much everywhere.

Sleep seems to be a tough battle for many women, but especially high-achievers. The wheels just never stop turning. I have to laugh now at the many ways colleagues and I discussed dealing with the never-ending ideas that come in the middle of the night. Those ideas would be the best ones that couldn't be lost!

I never really thought too much about the importance of a good night's sleep. In fact, I used to brag that I only needed five hours and I was good. Needless to say, eventually not getting proper rest took its toll. My weight suffered, my emotions suffered, my motivation suffered, and more. If I had those crazy busy corporate-job, family-raising years to do over, I would take more seriously getting a good night's sleep. Well, that would probably only work if I knew what I know now. Otherwise, I'm sure I would repeat the same mistakes. I've always had to learn things the hard way.

Naps are a good thing! Schedule time for a 15-minute nap at your desk. Put out the "do not disturb" sign, schedule a nap on your calendar and let nothing take its place. Put your head down and close your eyes for a few minutes. Many great leaders use naps to reenergize. You are great and you are a leader, so go for it! Don't believe the lie that you don't have time.

When it came to my physical wellness, I took a lot for granted. I am extremely blessed that I am relatively healthy, but when I look back, I now realize how much better I could have been in so many areas of my life had I focused on physical well-being more consistently. Certainly, there were times I tried to live healthier, but, honestly, it wasn't for the right reasons. To lose weight (comparing myself to others) was generally why I would go through times of giving exercise and better

Chapter 6
Self-Sabotage

eating my attention. And I lived in the quest of staying perpetually young.

Clearly, indulging in alcohol had its bad effects on my physical wellness too, adding extra calories and producing times when I felt too tired to exercise. Now, in my mid-50s, I look truth squarely in the eye and try to do what's best for my physical wellness. I am thankful we now live in a generation that sees the need for physical well-being.

Emotional wellness is directly affected by what we do to improve our physical health. I'm hoping this fact adds some incentive for you. Recognizing that our emotions must be cared for is a big deal. If we ignore this fact, we can easily end up turning to solutions we hope will provide instant relief or instant gratification. This is often when women turn to drinking, promiscuity, and other behaviors that create emotional bondage, which, in turn, produce secrets, and secrets are the worst thing for your emotional health!

Simple tips for emotional wellness begin with self-awareness. Know yourself and what your triggers are. If you know that every time you attend a budget meeting your blood pressure raises, then you want to prepare yourself. You can take five minutes before and after to meditate, take a quick walk, and say a prayer.

Do whatever works for you. If you need time to prepare for a meeting, put it on your schedule and make it a priority. Do not assume you will just have the time. In fact, don't assume anything except that you should prepare yourself.

In my corporate days, I had tons of meetings where the scheduling was out of my control. I would find myself in one meeting backed right up against another. Day after day, meetings upon meetings, I became emotionally drained. Most days I didn't think I had time for a break or for lunch, so I worked straight through. This was a bad idea. I can remember hearing the little voice in my head that said I should go to lunch with my co-workers and friends, but way too often I said, "No, I just don't have time." Eventually, this only added to the problems that drove my emotions downhill. I felt lonely and thought life was unfair. I was a victim of my own short-sided, professional and personal poor choices, but I couldn't see that at the time.

I got to a place where my emotions ran so high that I made way too many emotionally charged decisions. Decisions should never be made based on our emotions alone. While our emotions serve a purpose, that purpose gets lost when there isn't proper awareness. Proper awareness comes through maturity, maturity in knowing ourselves, maturity in our spirit, maturity in understanding that what we feel or what we think we see and hear is not always based on what is true, maturity

Chapter 6
Self-Sabotage

to find the truth before we make decisions or take action. Without maturity, the actions we take in an emotional state of mind almost always carry heavy consequences. Be aware that age is not an indicator of personal maturity.

For us gotta-it-all-going-on, high-achieving women, our emotions can easily be raw most of the time. Without good physical and spiritual well-being practices, we can simply get run down and lost in a life of self-sabotage.

Here are several important emotional well-being habits to practice when you feel your emotions running high:

1. Stop. Just stop and breathe.

2. Don't react.

3. Take time to assess what you know to be true in the situation.

4. Talk with a trusted person.

5. Determine if there is more information you need.

6. Respond based on what is true and, thus, appropriate.

The goal is to respond based on what is true and not to react based on your emotions. Repeat 3 times: "Respond; do not react," "Respond; do not react," "Respond; do not react."

Responding provides the opportunity for positive results. Reacting almost always brings with it less than favorable results, which, in turn, raises more emotional issues. Reacting hurts your integrity, whereas responding provides the opportunity to build integrity.

Spiritual wellness is the foundation for everything we've talked about so far. Without a spiritual base, we tend to wander in the wind. There are no two ways about it. Everyone has a soul, and our souls must be cared for. When I run out into my busyness day after day, my soul longs for rest and connection. When it doesn't get what, it needs, the result is a disconnect with who I am and why I am. I lose connection with my Creator, and thus I lose sight of my life purpose. Without connection to my life purpose, I'm easy prey for lonely and depressive states, because I start questioning if life is worth it. And then I may easily start believing foolish thoughts that my life doesn't really matter.

I highly encourage the building of solid spiritual well-being habits, which include daily prayer, meditation, and Scripture reading. Join a ladies' Bible study or put together a group and read a book together that will grow each member spiritually. There are many apps available that facilitate daily reading of the Scriptures.

If you need clarity around your life purpose, do your research. I offer this service in my life-coaching. There are many articles that can help with this as well. Many people don't think too much about their life purpose until mid-life. When the realization hits us that we are getting older and this life won't go on forever, we wonder if we shouldn't be doing more. Do we have a greater purpose than what we've been able to see and execute thus far? Knowing your purpose will bring great direction and meaning to your life. I encourage everyone to take the time of working through a God-directed, life-purpose process. The many blessings of doing this will knock your socks off!

Doing what is in front of you without clarity is a great saboteur. As an example, how often have you said, "I just want to be happy." And then you set out doing things you think will result in happiness. Yet you haven't defined what happiness really means to you. It's easy to go about making assumptions about what happiness is, but those things may never bring fulfillment. You and I must know what we are looking for.

Spirituality is a broad term and means different things to different people. I am a Christian, so spirituality to me means living the life God created me for. It means serving Jesus Christ my Savior. I recognize that there is a power greater than I and that my life has meaning beyond what I think I know. It means I love and serve others for a greater purpose. It means there is life beyond this world in which we live.

Although I did not grow up in church, I had some religious training in my childhood. In my early adult years, I thought religion was what I needed. That's all I knew; it was what I thought God was all about. I mentioned maturity when talking about emotional wellness. With spiritual maturity comes the understanding that religion exists, but it's not what we long for, nor is it what we are created for. A relationship of love is what my spirit, and yours, requires to be complete, whole, and well. That relationship is found in our Creator.

Overall wellness comes through physical, emotional, and spiritual wellness. This is what combats self-sabotage. So many things that appear to be part of our nature as strong women will be seen for what they really are when you practice overall wellness, things like:

- Controlling people

- Controlling circumstances

- Judging others

- Believing we have a right to revenge

- Seeking perfection

Chapter 6
Self-Sabotage

- Having unrealistic expectations

- Jealousy

- Constantly doing and never just being

- Trying to fix other people

The cycle of insanity where we return to the same stress-filled places repeatedly must stop. *Overall wellness* brings about the best you there is, the you that doesn't just dream about a life where you thrive daily, but the you who is thriving daily.

~

"Without good physical well-being habits and good spiritual well-being, we simply get run down and lost in a life of self-sabotage."

Awareness is Key

Identify Your Inner Conflicts of SELF-SABOTAGE

- ❖ In what ways, do you self-sabotage?

- ❖ What effects has your self-sabotage had on your life?

- ❖ What effects has your self-sabotage had on others?

Choose to THRIVE!

- ❖ Overcoming self-sabotage often requires the help of others. Seek trusted people to help you identify the changes you need to make and to stay accountable to healthy changes.

- ❖ Be honest with yourself.

- ❖ Never say the words "I can't help it," because you always have a choice.

- ❖ Ask others what self-sabotaging behaviors they see in you.

Chapter 7
Forgiveness

hard to forgive others,
harder to forgive myself

There are a lot of tough things in this world with which to deal. One of the toughest I've dealt with is finding it in my heart to forgive. I've struggled with both forgiving others and forgiving myself. The offenses to be forgiven have ranged from something minor such as rudeness or disrespect to what I would consider something quite major like harm done to one of my loved ones.

I've mentioned multiple times that high-achieving women have high expectations. I believe this is one of the reasons forgiveness is so difficult for us. We expect a lot from others and when our expectations are not met, we want people to be held accountable. We may see forgiveness as a demonstration of weakness, and, frankly, we desire that people pay for what they've done. The problem here is that we don't own that right. Unfortunately, however, we falsely believe that if we don't forgive them, then we are making them pay for what they did.

In my journey, I have found it easier to forgive others more so than to forgive myself. As high-achieving

Chapter 7
Forgiveness

women, we are clearly hard on ourselves. This includes the expectation that we can do better and that we shouldn't, or won't, give in to many of the temptations to which we see others succumb. This type of thinking caused me to believe that all I needed was enough will-power.

We all know the story from Matthew 7:24-27 about the man who built his house on sand and the one who build his house on solid ground. It didn't turn out so well for the man who built on sand. I discovered that will-power alone is one sandy beach that will not withstand high tide. Things I judged others for and said, "I would never do that," are the very things I fell to. It also applies to prideful belief that with enough will-power I could bury forgiveness issues and never have to deal with them. I thought that if I buried those issues deep enough and didn't talk about them, they would eventually go away. Wrong!

When I sold myself out to Jesus, I began a committed walk in recovery at the same time. I love how God orchestrated what He knew I needed, because the road was going to get rough before it got easier. I had a lot of spiritual newness and I became determined to learn and grow. I knew things in my life had to change and I was committed that they would. I realized that forgiveness would be tough, but I didn't know it would be one of the greatest stumbling blocks to my staying the course.

Asking for forgiveness

As I journeyed this new road with God, I took advantage of everything available my church had to offer. Looking back, I can see how being involved in multiple activities was critical. Over time, all of it worked together to soften my heart. Simultaneously, I gained an understanding that my sins were not less than or greater than the sins of anyone else. This was a key factor for me to get my head and heart wrapped around.

The first bridge I crossed related to forgiveness was making amends to others for things I had done. And let me tell you, I was scared to contact some of the people I had hurt. At the time, I was working through Rick Warren's book, The *Purpose Driven Life* (Warren 2012) which gave me ideas of how to go about making amends. I made phone calls, talked to people in person, and wrote letters. I was truly sorry and I hoped people would forgive me; most did.

It took me a while to fully grasp that I wasn't doing this to gain their forgiveness, but rather, I had to own what was mine. Ownership brings humility. Humility brings remorse for the pain we've caused others. Even in my fear, I could pour out my heart and genuinely express sorrow for the pain I had caused. This was the best I

Chapter 7
Forgiveness

could do. It was all I could do. I couldn't erase what had been done, but neither could I let the past own me and beat me up any longer.

You might be a little confused when I said that I wasn't doing this to gain their forgiveness. Here's the thing, when you apologize (try and make amends) to someone, they can choose to forgive you or not. If they don't forgive you, then what happens? Chances are high, you won't forgive yourself. You also won't allow the other person to own their decision not to forgive you because you will try to own it for them. This creates a constant cycle of beating yourself up. And this cycle has to stop.

Another side of forgiveness is the obvious of forgiving others. In recovery, we learn to make amends for our part (we own our stuff). We work through forgiving others, but with the understanding that we aren't doing it to let the other person "off the hook." Rather, we are doing it to free ourselves. Sooner or later, we come to an awareness that hanging on to the bitterness is only destroying ourselves. We allow God to soften our hearts, we obey His command to forgive, and we let it go.

This is one of the many reasons I love the recovery process and wish everyone would go through it. A person will never be whole and able to fully serve and love others until they deal with everything that's holding their heart in bondage. If the other person chooses to accept your amends and forgive you, then their heart will be set free as well. If they don't, that is their choice and you have to let them live with that. This all works the same whether your need is to forgive someone else or to forgive yourself.

It's a choice

Forgiveness is a decision, but, as previously stated, it's also a process that begins when you become willing to let God change your heart. That process is a journey that is unique to every person for every situation. I know the pain that never goes away from avoiding the decision or never working through the process. You know it too. It's that big black cloud that just gets darker and bigger the longer we try to avoid it. It's the anxiety and anger you feel when the memories come rushing back of what you or someone else has done.

In my journey of learning to walk with God and committing to life in recovery, there were many times I had to deal with the same forgiveness issues (meaning forgiveness isn't a one-time event) with both myself and others. For me, it was difficult to give myself any grace for the blatant selfish choices I had made. There is something about the guilt of disappointing those we love that is so difficult to get beyond.

Chapter 7
Forgiveness

Thankfully, not everything gets dealt with all at once. This is important if you believe the mountain of stuff you need forgiveness for is just too big. Only those things that God raises up in the present is what you need to focus on. Your over-achieving, impatient self may want everything dealt with all at once and done with, but that is a recipe for failure. Thankfully, God's pace is slow and steady. Getting through one forgiveness issue provides strength and courage for the next. Each one draws you closer to God, makes you stronger for your next step, and prepares your heart for bridges that will have to be crossed in the future.

I work with women on a lot of different issues, but at the top of the list is their inability to forgive themselves or others. Along with this comes the struggle of living with regrets. Forgiveness does not automatically remove them. Some people are haunted by regrets; in those cases, I believe that means forgiveness has not really occurred. When forgiveness has taken place, there is a deep, inner peace, a peace in which we choose to allow the regrets to have a helpful purpose.

Regrets bring back memories of time wasted, things missed out on, and, of course, people who got hurt, including ourselves. It is important to have an authentic awareness of our regrets because without clarity, regrets can easily take on a life of their own and turn into non-productive pain like shame and guilt. Regrets can be productive and helpful when we are humbled by them and recognize that our memories can give others hope. They also remind us of where we never want to go again. We can gain wisdom from regrets. If a regret is holding you down and causing you to stay stuck, you have a forgiveness issue that needs to be dealt with. Learning to forgive, while sometimes difficult to grab ahold of, is a powerful process.

Admittedly, there can be difficult things that happen, and forgiveness can seem impossible. For example, if someone were to harm one of my children or grand-children, it's going to be a tough road ahead. While this is true, hopefully the time will come when the door of my heart can be cracked open enough to allow God and His forgiveness to enter in. If not, bitterness will take root, and bitterness is an ugly beast that destroys people.

One thing that can make forgiving others so hard is a lack of clarity about forgiveness and trust. These two get tied together, but they are not one in the same. For-giveness is required because God tells us in Ephesians 4:32 we are to forgive just as He has forgiven us. And the blessing He provides when we are obedient to this command is peace and freedom. Trust, however, is not the same. We can forgive someone for their actions, but that doesn't mean we should trust them and possi-bly let them hurt us all over again. Forgiveness is a command; trust has to be earned. Rebuilding trust takes time and it doesn't happen by what someone

Chapter 7
Forgiveness

says. Consistent action proves trustworthiness. It is a good thing to say, "I forgive you, but I don't trust you yet."

Letting go is not easy

By now you might be saying, "I hear you, Debbie, but I just can't do it. You don't know what they did to me!" What I would say to you is that too many women continue to be miserable because they aren't willing to forgive. Quite often they are driven by the fear that the original pain will be felt again, maybe the person will repeat the same acts all over again. Unfortunately, forgiveness is no guarantee this won't happen. However, choosing not to forgive is a guarantee that you will continue to cause yourself pain. I also find that in a lack of forgiveness women believe they are hanging on to control, which is a misguided belief that they are governing the relationship between themselves and the other person. This simply isn't true. All too often this is a mind and heart game we play.

Letting go of bitterness and resentment isn't easy. Most of us want to see the other person hurt just as badly as they hurt us. This never works. Often the other person moves on and the one left hostage to the pain is you and me. And all the while we're telling ourselves that we are hurting them. It's a cycle of insanity!

Obsessing over the past produces nothing good. I am thankful for the life lesson that if I want to move on, I must forgive and let God take care of the rest. If I hang on to my poor choices, or the poor choices of others, I will never fully live up to my God-given purpose. A heart blocked with forgiveness issues simply can't thrive and be all it was designed to be.

Continued willingness

I mentioned at the beginning of this chapter that forgiveness begins with willingness.   It's a willingness that allows God to step in and do what only He can do in turning your heart to see things differently. If you can open your heart enough to let God in, He will take care of the rest. Once your heart has been softened, the process to let go of the pain begins. How long does it take? No one can say. God will take you at the pace that's needed.

Oftentimes, forgiving is a decision that has to be made over and over, every time the same issue stirs up unhealthy emotions. Because it's so easy to hang on to the emotions that cause us not to forgive, it takes continual willingness and effort to choose and travel the path of forgiveness. Granted, it can be a tough road, but a road that carries tons of freedom. Initially, you may not see or feel that freedom, but it will come. You

Chapter 7
Forgiveness

have to keep choosing this path no matter how long it takes or how hard it seems.

Learning to forgive released so many things inside of me, things that added no value whatsoever to my life or to anyone around me. I had let myself become hard-hearted. I struggled to show compassion or see the best in others. I held on to the past and tried to ensure others paid for their wrongs, which only added to the internal bondage I had chosen to live with. I did the same thing when it came to forgiving myself. I had to let go and understand that no one, including me, is beyond error, which, in turn, broke down many walls.

Forgiving yourself or others is a choice. I cannot emphasize enough that choosing to forgive and learning how to walk through the pain was one of the best things that ever happened to me. I pray this happens for you as well, and know over time it will, if you choose to forgive yourself and others.

~

"A heart blocked with forgiveness issues simply can't thrive and be all it was designed to be."

Awareness is Key

Identify Your Inner Conflicts of FORGIVENESS

- ❖ What bitterness and resentments are you holding on to?

- ❖ How has a lack of forgiving yourself affected your life?

- ❖ How has a lack of forgiving others affected your life?

Choose to THRIVE!

- ❖ Ask yourself daily, "Who do I need to forgive?"

- ❖ Ask God to change your heart and help you to be a forgiving person.

- ❖ Determine to believe God and leave revenge to Him.

- ❖ If you are struggling to forgive, do not just live with it; seek help from a trusted pastor, counselor, life coach, or therapist.

Chapter 8
Victim

never ending pity-party,
must be confronted

We've all heard about those who live with a victim mentality. My first thought when I heard this phrase was, "That's not me!" After a while, I wasn't so sure. Had I played the victim card from time to time? Yes, I had. Here are just a few statements I've made a time or two:

"I can't help that my biological father never gave me the time of day."

"I can't help that I have to work all the time."

"I can't help that I inherited the disease of addiction."

The list could be much longer, but need I mention more? What are your "I can't help" statements?

It's true there are things in life that are out of a person's control, but that doesn't make them a victim. Of my examples above, there are components within my control, but I believed they weren't. The factors that make up our lives can either be value-added and serve to make us stronger or we can let them pull us down and keep a black cloud over us. I've done both. The nature of the victim mentality is that I don't take ownership for

Chapter 8
Victim

my behaviors because things have happened to me that aren't my fault. It's a constant pity-party that wears people down.

In the days when I let the victim mentality have a life of its own within me, I was the classic case. I took ownership for almost nothing. It was easy to say things like, "I drink because I deserve to relax," or "I have to work all the time because money doesn't grow on trees," or "I'm overweight because I don't have time to work out," and the list goes on. We seem to have a ton of reasons, but in every case, somebody else or something is to blame.

Time to take ownership

We all have choices, but when playing the victim, it is easier to just stay on the surface of our circumstances. Ownership means going deep and being vulnerable. I would have to dig into what was driving me to make certain choices and take responsibility for a tougher and harder road. Staying on the surface was simply easier and kept me comfortable in my dysfunctional behaviors.

What an oxymoron: "...kept me comfortable in my dysfunctional behaviors." Such a statement sounds so contradictory, but it really isn't. There is comfort in the status quo, no matter how much one may become aware that the status quo is doing them no favors. Even when you realize that staying in the same behaviors is unhealthy and holding you back, it may not be enough for you to do something about it. Unhealthy behaviors can range from gossip to a lack of forgiveness to gluttony to alcohol abuse to lying to cheating to codependency to _____ (fill in the blank). It's a long list.

Change requires moving into new territory. But what will my life be like if I change? Who will I be? How will this or that work? For me, when I reached this point, I didn't like who I had become, but that person kept me at my comfort level, good or bad. I had been in my dysfunction for so long that I could not comprehend who I would be or what life would be like outside of it. I became afraid I wouldn't know how to do life anymore. For a self-sufficient, high-achieving woman, this is scary. I hated being controlled by alcohol, but I was scared to death of what life would be like without it. I hated trying to control everything and everyone around me, but I was scared to death to let go.

I spent many years blaming others for the dysfunctional choices I made. I blamed my husband because he couldn't live up to my expectations. I blamed my job because I had too much on my plate. I blamed bosses because they added stress to my life. I blamed peers because they weren't carrying their part of the load. I blamed my ex-husband because he chose not to pay child support. I blamed my dead-beat biological father. I blamed God because He could have made it all different. Playing the victim was all too easy.

When I first heard of the victim mentality, because I considered myself strong and in control, I didn't buy into it. I justified my right to keep believing and thinking others were the source of my problems.

Thankfully, God never gave up on me. I was not aware of His pursuit at the time, but looking back I can see how He was always there. Coming to the end of myself to see Him and allow Him into my heart took much longer than I like to admit. He gave me plenty of opportunities; I simply wanted life on my terms, which left little room for Him and His ways. This is critical because I needed to see that nobody but me had responsibility for how I chose to respond to the things that had happened to me and around me. I learned that taking ownership for our responses is what disarms the victim mentality.

Playing the victim keeps your pain and the relative dysfunctional behaviors alive. I do not mean to make light of horrible situations that may have occurred in people's lives, especially situations where the true definition of being a victim has occurred. I do mean to say that at some point, you have to own whether you move forward or stay stuck. I am also not suggesting that moving forward is easy. Every situation is different. But even when we are true victims, the time comes when we have a decision to make. Thankfully I have personally crossed this bridge. Eventually, I had to decide if I would set myself free from the pain by forgiving my perpetrator or continue to justify the hate in my heart.

The victim role comes in many forms. It can begin as a true victim situation such as rape or a father who never cared enough to know the child he took part in making. It can come from finding yourself in an abusive relationship or staying in a job where you feel trapped. It can be rooted in a belief system imposed on you by others or through head games you've learned to play.

Regardless of the source, you have to confront the victim mentality by taking ownership that you are the one in control of every choice you make. Be the author of your life. Own your choices and stop believing the lies that other people and/or circumstances are an excuse for unhealthy behaviors or staying in a miserable place.

When I started owning things, like how I would view the fact that I inherited alcoholism, big changes began. I accepted the fact that I inherited this disease, but I also accepted the fact that owning it means I can let it kill me or I can choose to overcome it. I accept the fact that I've never known my biological father and I can let that fact kill me with bitterness or I can choose to overcome it and be a better, stronger person because of it.

Chapter 8
Victim

For everything that tries to bring us down, we have a choice to make. The victim mentality tells us there is no choice and we must live a painful existence. Taking ownership says we always have a choice and that we choose the road of opportunity and growth *because of* the imperfect things in our lives.

Most high-achieving women would never believe they've played the victim card. I would ask you to look deeper. This book is all about seeing where our assets have turned bad and seeing character defects that have crept in. Awareness is key to overcoming these factors. Seeing ourselves as victims, even victims of ourselves, is one of those things that can easily creep into our belief system. Our response to the things that have happened in our lives determines whether we reap blessings or wallow in some form of self-pity.

~

"We all have choices, but when playing the victim, it is easier to just stay on the surface of our circumstances. Ownership means going deep and being vulnerable."

Awareness is Key

Identify Your Inner Conflicts of playing the VICTIM

❖ How do you feel about owning your choice of response even in a situation where the other person committed a terrible offense against you?

❖ Are you playing the victim role in any area of your life? If so, how is this impacting you? How might it be impacting others around you?

❖ What do you need to own or forgive to put an end to playing the victim?

Choose to THRIVE!

❖ Don't assume that you *never* play the victim card.

❖ Get clear on what playing a victim looks like within yourself and deal with the root cause(s) of why you tend to go there.

❖ Don't play into the unhealthy behaviors of others who play the victim role.

❖ Remember that playing the victim is a choice.

Chapter 9
Perfection

easy to desire,
impossible to attain

High expectations are a staple for high-achieving women. We expect much to be done and we expect it to be done right. Dare I say, we expect things to be done perfectly?

I have lived with the burden of striving for perfection ever since I can remember. It is still the number one character flaw I battle (I'm sure there are others that my loved ones would be happy to tell you about!). One of the hardest things about perfectionism is identifying it. I have discovered that this little joy robber disguises itself in many ways.

When I was starting my coaching business, about six years ago, as of this writing, I wrestled with everything from feeling like an imposter, because I was new to the profession of life-coaching, to constantly believing my website wasn't good enough. You name it and I wrestled with it. I worried, cried, and even had on hand medication for anxiety. It was bad. Worse yet, this went on for over a year! Self-imposed stress was way over the top. I wanted to quit so many times because I was just sure that I would never be "ready."

Chapter 9
Perfection

I realize that much of what I was feeling has been felt by many an entrepreneur. For me, it became almost paralyzing. I must have drove people around me crazy as I was continually walking in this fear of being able to do everything the right way and wanting to be *good enough*. I was frightened of asking people to pay for my services, and what if they didn't find their path forward? What if their lives didn't improve? What if, what if, what if! At times, the thoughts were awful and debilitating. Perfectionism had me wanting to be the god in people's lives!

I have to go down a little side road here. When I did my life-coach training, I was diligent about my research. I wanted to pick a good school and I wanted a thorough program. No "six weeks to being a life coach" for me. Perhaps I was looking for the perfect school, although I believe my real goal was to ensure I came out the other side with the knowledge and practicums that would make me a good coach for serving God's people. My training was from the Christian Coaching Institute and it was a year-long program. I did not miss classes; I completed all my assignments; and I participated fully. However, when it came time to be in business for myself, I panicked. Suddenly, nothing was good enough. Never mind all the training, practicum work, past experience I had under my belt. I was blinded. That is what striving for perfectionism can do.

No such thing as perfection

One day, I took advantage of a free offer by a well-known coach in the Christian coaching community. As I talked with her, it came to me that the root issue I struggled with was trying to be perfect. I couldn't believe that I had put myself through so much pain for over a year, which, in turn, stagnated my business. I finally saw how I had wanted to have the perfect website, the perfect set of coaching forms, the perfect ability to coach others, the perfect program, and on and on. I was beating myself up over something that isn't even possible! There is no such thing as the perfect way to do anything. There is the experience of what has worked for some and what has worked for others, but that doesn't make either of them perfect.

This was all very eye-opening because before that I had never really focused on the issue of perfectionism. What I discovered as I prayed and looked back over my life is that being a perfectionist was huge in me. When I really looked at this, I found it *everywhere*. Not only did I expect it from myself, but I expected it from others as well.

So, the above confession is something you already gathered about me from the chapter that talked about my crazy Sergeant Mom days. Let me go ahead right now and confess another ugly, true story of how perfectionism has not served me or others well.

Chapter 9
Perfection

I am a person who loves new organizations. I love the work of pulling together a team, writing policies and procedures, establishing workflow, interviewing candidates, and all the tasks that go with ensuring an organization runs productively and efficiently. I know it's kind of sick, but, hey, somebody has to do it!

I've started and/or led many organizations in my time. Picture a person who loves this kind of work, but also wants it done *perfectly*. Do you have any idea how many procedures for those procedures for those procedures that can be developed when the mindset is *perfection*? Can you imagine the pain to the people who have to follow all those procedures? Can you say, "Nightmare?" I can remember efforts in my corporate days when I drove my organization crazy trying to keep up with all the procedures to ensure we did everything right. While I know, I have learned from that craziness, I still have to watch myself, because I can easily jump to, "We need a procedure for that!" Of course, procedures are a good thing, but when the motive is because I want to be *perfect*. That's not good.

It's important to recognize that perfectionism abounds and largely goes undetected. Yet, it is the underlying source for much of the stress many people live with.

In no way am I suggesting that we shouldn't always be about doing the best job we can. But to think that a mistake will never happen and we should constantly strive to be perfect is simply not realistic, and it tears people down. People cannot relax into being passionate, creative, and fully motivated when they are worried about meeting perfectionist standards.

The culprit of perfectionism

I can see how my perfectionism has stolen years off my life. I felt pressure to have the perfect house with perfect stuff, to be fully knowledgeable and fully involved in every project my team worked on, to run myself ragged to meet every deadline and make every appointment, to look perfect with my clothes, jewelry, shoes, purses, to constantly worry if others were going to do their part perfectly, to be everything to everyone. The list of areas that perfectionism can take hold is endless. When the situations in these areas are, all occurring at the same time, the stress will take years off a person's life.

So, what do we do? Perfectionism is a sneaky beast and hard to tame in high-achieving women. We take ownership seriously in our many roles and we take pride in doing things well. None of that is bad. What we have to watch out for is driving ourselves, our families and the people we lead by unrealistic expectations.

Chapter 9
Perfection

It takes a conscious effort to step back and look at what we are asking for. Does it leave room for people, including ourselves, to do what they do best? Or does it pigeonhole them into doing things the way we think is best? Do people believe they have the latitude to take calculated risks without harsh repercussions? Do you give yourself grace when you mess up? Do you give your child grace when they don't do as well as you think they should have? Are we leaving room for God to work?

Expecting perfection from the people around you will cause them to eventually leave. They will either get tired of the pressure or they will see no point in their efforts because they can't meet what you want. Remember the chapter on loneliness. Perfectionism results in loneliness.

Put others first

One of the best ways to fight letting perfectionism drive you is to exercise the important leadership skill of putting people first. Putting people first is about loving others and a heartfelt desire to always add value to others. When you do this, you will look at things from their perspective and not just your own concerns that are naturally present when you are in charge of the business at hand. This includes practicing this same skill with yourself. A leader who does not lead themselves well will not lead others well.

I have passed the character defect of perfectionism to some of my children. I hear their pain as they simply "try to do their best." My prayer is for them to fully recognize the difference between a healthy desire to be their best with their God-given abilities and wanting to be perfect.

A healthy desire puts God first and the motivation is about His glory. Perfectionism is always about one's self, but that can be hard to see.

~

"People cannot relax into being passionate, creative, and fully motivated when they are worried about meeting perfectionist standards."

Chapter 9
Perfection

Awareness is Key

Identify Your Inner Conflicts of PERFECTION

- ❖ Where do you see, perfectionism having its way in your life?

- ❖ What issues has perfectionism caused you and those you love?

- ❖ How do you currently deal with your perfection-ist tendencies?

Choose to THRIVE!

- ❖ Do not be fooled. Perfectionism disguises itself in "just wanting to get things done right." Take time to reflect.

- ❖ Ease up. Truth is that the world will not fall apart if things aren't done exactly as you think they should be.

- ❖ Allow yourself and people to make mistakes. It's the best learning tool we have. Grace goes a long way.

- ❖ Focus on adding value to people through nur-turing relationships and giving them room to grow.

Chapter 10
Transformation

intentional decisions,
an intentional journey

Finally, I did something right! Truth be told, I've done many things right in my life. I don't say that to brag, but rather to expound on the truth of the opening statement; there's been more than just one thing. One (actually five) of the things I am so grateful and proud of is my children. They are all wonderful adults who bring me great joy. By the grace of God, three of them have all grown into awesome parents who have given my husband and me 10 (as of this writing) wonderful grandchildren. We also have one great-grandchild thus far who is just as awesome as he can be. My youngest two do not have children yet, but if they do, they too demonstrate characteristics of being great parents.

The "something" I was referring to in the first sentence is when I finally committed my life to Jesus. I mean, I sold myself out to Him. I tried many avenues to be free from the turmoil I carried around inside for so long. God was an avenue I had tried off and on. I had also tried to find relief in my family, friends, work, substances, food, and more. All of them worked for a short period, but when the newness wore off, I found that all my internal struggles were still there.

Chapter 10
Transformation

I thought that if I could find happiness, then I would be free of the constant turmoil inside me. I spent years trying to put on a happy face and find that one thing that would deliver me. I realize now that happiness is a state of mind, an emotion generally driven by circumstances. I spent years trying to find it as though it were a destination I could reach, a fix that would suddenly make me a truly whole and complete person.

Finding true happiness

I was not raised in church, but I knew there was a God. The problem for most of my life is that God was more of a concept to me than a reality. I absolutely did not understand that believing in God and believing the truth of His word are two very different things. To me, the Bible was a history book containing strange stories inapplicable to current times.

I also did not understand that having a relationship with God was what "church" was all about. Honestly, I spent many years thinking that if I went to church on Sunday, I was good and that heaven would be waiting for me when the time came. I went to church because I thought that's what I was supposed to do. I sent my kids to parochial school because I wanted them to have a "better education" and be in an environment where they would be taught about God.

Chapter 10
Transformation

There were some spots in the timeline of my life where I reached out to God in a very real way. Each time I opened my heart to Him, but then I would get scared and pull away. I feared losing my life as I knew it. I was never ready to give all of myself to Him, so I went right back to the same me, fighting my same battles.

People say that Satan is never more active than in a home on Sunday mornings. I couldn't agree more. Then he is right back at it within minutes after we walk out of church. When my kids were growing up, the fighting that went on to get everybody ready and out the door was crazy. The fighting before we got out of the parking lot to head home was even crazier! I bet there were only a handful of times I could have told you what the sermon was about later in the day. My obligation, as far I was concerned, was to attend church and repeat some standard prayers. This left little room for God to have any real impact on my life. It also kept the door wide open for Satan to walk through.

My husband was raised in church. He knew what a relationship with Jesus meant and he loves the Lord. For quite a few years, however, he had placed God on a shelf. I only include this to say that we wandered in the wilderness of not walking with or serving the Lord for a quite a while. And I did little to help change this.

I remember a couple of times when I was trying to put my old life behind me and walk a new path. One of

111

Chapter 10
Transformation

those times, my husband helped lead me to Christ. I prayed the sinner's prayer and distinctly remember an almost out-of-body experience. I knew without a doubt that God heard my prayer and that I was His. That was awesome, and my walking close to Him lasted for almost a year and a half.

The problem with each time I tried to rededicate my life and walk with Jesus, and there were several of these times over the years, was that I still wanted to do things my way. I hadn't accepted that I had a drinking problem, that I was controlling, that I was arrogant, that I was selfish, that I worshipped money, that I worshipped myself.

I wanted a relationship with Jesus, but I either didn't understand or didn't want to understand that in this relationship He is King. I would have to allow Him to constantly show me the things in my character and in my life, that had to go, things that kept me from being the person He created me to be. I had no idea who that person was, how to find her, or even that I should be looking for her.

I finally tried His way

I was 45 years old before I fully surrendered and tried life His way. Prior to this, I would seek God every few years when I was at the end of my rope and I didn't know what else to do. I was finally recognizing that I couldn't have it my way on most days and His way on some. That's just not how Jesus works. He wanted all of me and I had not been willing to give myself completely to Him. The Bible says, "You cannot serve both God and money [or two Gods]" (Matthew 6:24, NIV). I was my own god, alcohol was my god, money was my god, my career was my god, my children were my gods, my husband was my god, and much more. Not one of these things can come before Jesus, but I tried to make them coexist as Lord of my life for way too long. I didn't think I was putting anything "before" God, but when those things took priority over Him and His will for my life, that's exactly what I was doing.

At the height of my dysfunction, my husband and I separated. We had been separated for a year when I sold myself out to Jesus. Also now, I was several months into rehabilitation from a badly broken leg. Interestingly, this turned out to be the blessing I needed to let God into my heart.

I had not been drinking to get drunk in a quite a while, but on one Saturday night, I did. I remember it like it was yesterday. I had been attending church regularly by now. But on that Sunday, I pulled into the church parking with no intention of going in. I was only there to pick up one of my children who had spent the night with a friend. The minute I pulled into the parking lot, it was as though God was sitting in the car with me. I heard a voice that said, "It's time to get off the fence." That's it. That's all He said. "It's time to get off the fence."

My mind was a bit clouded, but somehow, I knew it was the voice of God and I knew what He meant. No longer could I play the games I had been playing, trying to live my way *and* His way. The battle of good and evil that raged inside for years had to end. So, I went into church that morning. I went up front at the altar call and committed my life to Jesus. And I desired to be baptized.

Many people have heard me tell this story. I add that if you had seen me that day you would know how true this story is, because had I known I was going up in front of the church that morning, I would have dressed better! Wearing sweats to church is not my style. I don't care what anyone else wears; I'm just telling you that's not what I wear.

The next week I met with my minister and he helped me be clear about the commitment I was making. The following week my eldest son baptized me. That was two weeks after my 45th birthday, and my life has never been the same. Little did I know that I would hear from God again soon and another big message would follow.

"Call your husband..."

Two weeks after being baptized, God spoke once again. This time He said, "Call your husband and put your marriage back together." Immediately, I said out loud (I was in my home by myself), "Oh, I can't do that!" However, somehow, I knew that I was making a decision that would have *big* consequences with it as soon as those words came out of my mouth. It was going to impact many people, but I didn't recognize that truth in that moment.

Before I could talk myself out of it, I picked up the phone and made the call. I hadn't even thought about what I was going to say. I just knew that I had to do what God had told me to do. To say I was scared is a serious understatement. That single, intentional act of obedience was the start of an awareness that God is greater than my fears. I discovered so many things as I traveled this new road with God, and I came to realize that it all started with that first choice to obey Him and get off the fence.

- I learned that nothing is as hard as I can cook it up in my mind to be.

- I learned that even if the response by the other person is not what I hope for, I am going to be okay.

Chapter 10
Transformation

- I learned that God has a plan and I don't need to worry about the whole plan; I just need to do what He places in front of me.

- I learned what it means to step out in faith.

- I learned what it means to trust.

- I learned what it means to act in the courage that He provides.

- I learned that He always has a plan, and even though I can't see it that doesn't make it any less so.

- I learned that the silence of God is not the absence of God.

You are probably wondering what my husband said when I made the call. He didn't respond favorably. In fact, he said, "I don't think so." Thankfully, he knew the voice of God and he heard Him right after hanging up the phone. It didn't happen overnight, but we did reconcile. It took another year for us to work through things. During that time, I heard God say that my marriage would not only come back together, but also that it would be stronger than it had ever been. I hung on to that message many, many times when I wanted to walk away and say, "Forget it!" I became intentional daily by continuing to put God's plan first in my life over my will and what I wanted to do.

Within a few months of our reconciliation, my husband and I became part of the ministry leaders for Celebrate Recovery at our church. We still lead that ministry today. Subsequently, our family found forgiveness between one another and grew in ways I could never have imagined. To say we became "stronger than we had ever been" is absolute truth.

Just trust Him

When I look back at how God worked His plan, a plan that only He could fully see, I am in awe. When I think about how many times my husband or I could have walked away from putting one foot in front of the other and trusting that God knew what He was doing, it melts my heart. I am so grateful for doing this right, for listening and obeying. The strength and power to do so came from God Himself. I had tried it my way so many times, and it never came close to working. God always has a plan and He sees the path ahead that we cannot yet fathom. He only asks that we trust Him.

Transformation has resulted in the elimination of many internal struggles that kept me bound for most of my life. When I finally got intentional about not letting the

Chapter 10
Transformation

fear of change drive me away from God, my whole world turned around. Transformation requires that we walk through the sources of our discomfort.

The result of intentionally seeking transformation has been all those things I longed for and thought I was always striving to reach:

- peace and contentment

- a genuine love for others

- love for myself

- restored relationships

- living out my life purpose; the impact He created and designed me for

- self-confidence in who God created me to be

This "something done right" changed my life and had incredible effects on those I love the most. I am not taking all the credit for this by any stretch. God works in me every day to continue following the right path. It's not easy at times to put my high-achieving self aside when I believe she needs to rise up and live life on her terms. I will always be a work in progress.

I have to make a conscious choice to be intentional in the decisions I make multiple times every day. I still do things without thinking it through. When I do, the results are what I've seen in a past: inner turmoil and strife. I don't ever want to go back there! The good news about this is that it keeps me in a place of humility and not falsely thinking I've conquered my humanness. Without mistakes, we lose our ability to have open hearts that allow God to grow and mature us into the people He will use to accomplish His great plan. We are here by His design for His purposes.

You, too, can have transformation wherever you need it in your life. High-achieving women are a great gift to this world. We can also be our own worst enemies. Mostly, we approach things in life intentionally. Transformation is no different. In fact, it absolutely requires our greatest intentionality. The steps to transformation will work if you work them:

- Own your struggles so you can get to the root cause.

- Once you are clear on the root cause(s) that need to be dealt with, discuss them with a trusted professional, pastor, counselor, life coach, or therapist.

- Put a plan in place and march to that plan with great accountability (see Chapter 11).

Chapter 10
Transformation

- Admit that you are not the one in control; seek God and His plan for your life.

~

"Transformation requires that we walk through the sources of our discomfort."

Awareness is Key

Identify Your Inner Conflicts of
TRANSFORMATION

- ❖ Are you avoiding a transformation God wants to make in your life? How so?

- ❖ What are your fears about letting go and letting God transform you?

- ❖ What will it take to allow the transformation to occur?

Choose to THRIVE!

- ❖ Believe that transformation is not near as scary as we make it out to be.

- ❖ Get started on one healthy change TODAY.

- ❖ Reconcile the truth that nothing changes if nothing changes. You can let fear rule and keep you from what you know you need to do.

- ❖ Seek a trusted resource to partner with you in your transformation journey.

Chapter 11
Boundaries

the need for boundaries,
the need for accountability

Setting and maintaining boundaries is one of my favorite topics. I have learned the hard way how important healthy boundaries are and how rough life can be when boundaries either don't exist or are not being adhered to if they have been established.

Boundaries make it clear to me and to others who I am, where I draw the lines. I must be extremely clear on this myself before I can implement and expect anyone else to respect my boundaries. I must know what I will allow and what I will not allow, what I like and what I dislike. If I am not clear myself about where I stand, there is no way I can expect anyone else to be.

Boundaries come in both physical and non-physical. Physical boundaries are much easier to identify: don't cross this line; don't smoke in my house; don't come into my office when the "I can't be interrupted" sign is out. Non-physical boundaries are much tougher: I do not like profanity; I do not gossip; I will have protected quiet time to pray every day.

Chapter 11
Boundaries

Setting my boundaries

Boundaries must be identified, implemented, and adhered to by everyone, first, within themselves. When I got sick and tired of being miserable, driven by a myriad of things, I did something about it that I knew was a healthy approach. I mentioned previously that not everything wrong in my life had to be dealt with at once, and I thank God for that. I just needed to start somewhere with intentional boundaries that would serve my life well rather than result in even more internal pain and conflict.

When I decided to give my life to Jesus Christ, I knew I had to decide what that would look like. If I didn't, the result would be the same as all the other times I committed to walk with God but then fell away. And each time I fell away brought another round of guilt and condemnation.

My boundaries were to make prayer and learning who God is a priority. I prayed diligently and I did much more than just attend church on Sundays. I was in a place where I needed more and knew it. I joined a women's Bible study and a small group at my church. These were two things I had never done before, ever. I did not miss attending or doing any of the homework outside of group even when I had to force myself. Each day,

124

my prayer time was protected by getting up earlier before anyone else in my house. I adhered to my boundaries and engaged others to help me stay accountable.

When I first got serious about my recovery from alcohol, I set boundaries, such as not going into bars and not going in the door at the grocery store that took me right past the liquor. You may wonder if I attended AA meetings. At this point, I did not. That was also a boundary for me. I knew I wasn't in a place to deal with local meetings where I lived. Some of those meetings were not safe (at least for me), and there were people I knew there that could be triggers. Additionally, because I was fully engaged with growing spiritually, I now had a place to heal and grow within the church.

I am not suggesting this course of action for everyone; this is what worked for me. I have now been attending recovery meetings almost weekly since we started Celebrate Recovery (12-plus years ago, as of this writing). The important point is to identify what you must do to stay the course of transformation to which you've committed.

What do those boundaries look like? Once you are clear, implement them and have people hold you accountable. Accountability is key to knowing you are not alone, that people care for you, and that you have a solid support system when the going gets tough.

Chapter 11
Boundaries

The two areas of boundaries I've mentioned, spirituality and recovery, are two I faithfully maintain to this day. They have also brought forth the greatest transformations in my life.

We all need boundaries

Setting boundaries is not always easy. Having said that, it is to live in denial if you believe you don't need them. Having relationship issues or being stressed, overweight, down in spirit, angry, bitter, critical, discontent, and more result from a lack of good healthy boundaries. Is it time for you to stop the madness? If so, read on!

The practical steps to establishing boundaries begin with getting very real about what is going on. Perception is not reality. You have to get honest about what is driving the issues in your life. For example, when my use of alcohol became a problem in my life, for the most part, I blamed it on other people and circumstances. Even when I knew I was over-indulging, to admit that I was the problem was hard. Getting to the root is required to determine proper boundaries. But it's difficult, because being honest is not always easy and often gets clouded by our misguided justifications.

I am not trying to sell you on life-coaching, but I would be remiss if I did not share that setting boundaries is an excellent area in which to utilize a coach. A good life coach will help you dig deep and get real. They will help you establish boundaries that support what is best for you and help you maintain them. I will also say that problems can run deep and sometimes you need to utilize a counselor or therapist to find the root. A good life coach will not try to lead you when a different kind of professional might be a better choice.

Once you've identified the root cause of your life issues, setting the boundaries for healthy improvement requires that you do some soul searching about what you are willing to do. Without this, there really is no point in setting boundaries, because the likelihood is slim that you will stay strong when your boundaries are violated.

You need to determine if you will really confront your co-worker about their abuse of your time. You need to determine if you are willing to join a Bible study and stick with it if you want to grow and walk closer with God. You need to determine if you will stick to your guns and not let your child hang out with those kids you don't approve of.

For each boundary, you want to set, you must play out in your mind and heart what you are willing to do when the time comes when that boundary is challenged and you need to uphold it. Of course, you can't know for sure until you cross that bridge, but if you prepare yourself in advance to the best of your ability, you are doing what you can to set yourself up for success. You have to also think through what will happen in the heat of the battle if you don't uphold the boundary. If you can't stick to it, you are better off not to set it. When someone sees that you aren't serious about the boundaries you've set, it tells them your boundaries don't need to be respected. It then becomes hard to turn that situation around.

Once you have good boundaries in place, you want to get help sticking to them. Don't fool yourself into thinking that just because you put your boundaries out there everyone will adhere to them. It's only a matter of time before tough situations will come. Having strong people around you are important, people who will challenge your thinking and help you see why you set a boundary in the first place.

When it comes to boundaries with people we love and care about, maintaining the boundary will get difficult if they violate it. Our heart kicks in and tells us that if we loved them, we would let them _____ (fill in the blank). The truth is that we should be real about what loving someone means. It does not mean allowing bad or unhealthy behavior. This is true for ourselves as well. We've all heard it said that we have to love ourselves to love other people. I will not love myself if I continue to indulge in bad or unhealthy behavior. The two cannot coexist.

Good accountability partners are people with a strong spiritual foundation who can be objective, and who are willing to say the hard things when you need to hear them. Your best friend or closest family member may not be the best accountability partner. Engage as many accountability partners as you deem necessary, some-one to keep you accountable to attending meetings, one for staying strong with that co-worker, and one for keeping your work hours in check, for example. Decide what will work best. Then pray and seek out people to help you.

It's not about being selfish

Our ability to *thrive* in this fast-paced, all-too-busy world in which we live requires that we have strong boundaries and that we adhere to them. There are those who will believe your boundaries are mean or un-fair, or that you're being selfish. Everything in life comes down to the motives of your heart. If you deter-mine that you will spend fewer hours at work to honor your family values, is that selfish? Your boss could ac-cuse you of being selfish because there are projects that need your expertise to complete them on time. Your family might even say you are selfish because

Chapter 11
Boundaries

you could make more money if you would put in over-time. In these possible scenarios, if your motive supports what God has called you to, who He created you to be and thus, your core values, there's nothing selfish about it. Don't be swayed because others choose to see things their way.

I mentioned in a previous chapter that every high-achieving woman has to look at her life and determine what is truly necessary and what can be eliminated. There are always things that can either be eliminated or handled differently. This, too, is a great use of life coaches. They are trained to help you see things that you simply can't see because you are in the deep end of the pool swimming for your life. When you are drowning, something must change. Don't fall into the superwoman trap. She's not real!

"The practical steps to establishing boundaries begin with getting very real about what is going on. Perception is not reality."

Awareness is Key

Identify Your Inner Conflicts of BOUNDARIES and ACCOUNTABILITY:

- ❖ What boundaries have you been avoiding?

- ❖ What results have you seen in your life of not having solid healthy boundaries?

- ❖ What will it take to implement and/or adhere to the boundaries you need to THRIVE daily?

Choose to THRIVE!

- ❖ Utilize a trusted professional (pastor, counselor, life coach, therapist) to help you with clarity and proper boundary setting.

- ❖ Maintain your relationship with the professional until you are strong in adhering to your boundaries across tough opposition.

- ❖ Use accountability partners everywhere you can.

- ❖ Be very cautious of thinking, "I've got this," and letting go of accountability.

Chapter 11
Boundaries

❖ Assess your boundaries, minimally every six months, to ensure your motives are pure and the boundaries are still healthy.

Conclusion
Thrive

"Every woman that finally figured out her worth has picked up her suitcases of pride and boarded a flight to freedom, which landed in the valley of change." – Sharon L. Alder *(Alder n.d.)*

High-achieving women make this world go around. When we aren't able to thrive, it impacts us, but it also impacts others in a big way. I think we easily underestimate how much God uses us in other people's lives.

We are world-changers! God did not give us the skills and abilities we have to keep them to ourselves. When we aren't thriving, however, we aren't able to excel in fulfilling our God-ordained impact; life purpose.

Thriving isn't about more pressure; it's about an honest walk with God that takes us to incredible heights as high-achieving women. It's about seeing life from His eyes and living out His plan for us. This is true at work, in our communities, within our churches, and certainly with our family and friends.

In Chapter 1, I stated: "God had a plan, but I didn't find that out until 30 years later." Over my 30-year career, one thing I said quite often was that I wanted to stay home with my children. In the early years, I was always seeking a way to make that happen. Little did I know that God began early on saving me from myself. Let's face it, as a high-achieving woman, I am not the-stay-at-home mom type. And that is not a character defect. It's the way I am created. Many high-achieving woman are stay-at-home moms. We are each created for our individual purpose.

In later years, as my children got older, my statement changed to: "I want to retire when I have 30 years of service because I will only be 48 years old." Jokingly, I said this a lot, never ever believing it would happen. But it did happen. I remember the last day I worked in my office. I was on my knees, humbled, crying, and praying, because I couldn't believe my years of corporate work were really coming to an end. After all, working was a huge part of my identity. I had been doing it since I was 14 years old, starting in a local grocery store, and then by the time I was 18, working in a corporate environment.

As I prayed before entering my office, God impressed upon me a statement and a flashback. I heard Him say, "I kept you there." Then, in my mind's eye, I saw the timeframe when I went through my divorce. I don't know what I would have done without my job in those days to care for my children and provide us a home. Next, I saw the two times that I had tried to quit my job and how, both times, I realized I wasn't supposed to leave.

God's plan was that I stay and get my 30 years in. I believe this for many reasons. The opportunities to learn and grow in that environment were priceless. The ways in which He has used that learning to further my life purpose and impact others is amazing. I've been blessed with the kind of real-life experiences to help women through their poor life choices and come out victorious on the other side – and to leave their internal bondage behind them.

"Inner conflicts" can still come up. I still run into emotional loneliness, insecurities, discontentment, perfectionism. The difference between high-achieving women who thrive and those who don't is not the absence of "inner conflicts." Rather, it is not ignoring what should be dealt with, mistakes we've made or character traits that don't serve us well. We have a heart that chooses to respond to the prompting of God. Thus, we continually grow in His likeness and we take the steps of faith to live out the impact in this world that we were created for. This is the key to thriving in life, rather than just having a desire to thrive.

In his book, Soulprint, Mark Patterson states; "Most of us live our entire lives as strangers to ourselves. We know more about others than we know about ourselves. Our true identities get buried beneath the mistakes we've made, the insecurities we've acquired, and the lies we've believed. We're held captive by

Conclusion
Thrive

others' expectations. We're uncomfortable in our own skin. And we spend far too much emotional, relational, and spiritual energy trying to be who we're not." (Batterson 2011)

My prayer for you is found in 2 Thessalonians 3:5: "May the Lord lead your hearts into a full understanding and expression of the love of God and the patient endurance that comes from Christ" (NLT).

Thank you for expending your resources to read this book. Thank you for all that you are and for all that you do. You are an inspiration and a role model to all around you. The world could not thrive without you!

More for Your Thriving Life

One Life to THRIVE
Retreats and Community for
Women Who Lead

In the foothills of the Colorado Rocky Mountains is a place so serene. Glen Eyrie castle, "The Glen," is a world of its own where the presence of God is strong and alive.

One Life to THRIVE retreats focus on 3 areas:

> ➤ **CONNECT**ing with yourself God and others,

> ➤ **TRANSFORM**ing those inner struggles,

> ➤ **IMPACT**ing as God created and designed you for.

Beyond the retreats, One Life to THRIVE offers a community of like-minded women. Left to our own thoughts and busy lives, we will have a very difficult time maintaining the encouragement, focus, and strength to carry forth in the area(s) of impact we are created and designed for.

Ecclesiastes 4:9-10 states: "Two people are better off than one, for they can help each other succeed. If one

More for Your Thriving Life

person falls, the other can reach out and help. But someone who falls alone is in real trouble."

Do not stifle the passions of your heart. Join the movement of women choosing to step into the impact God created and designed them for! For more information visit: http://onelifetothrive.org

Life and Leadership Coaching

Coaching is an amazing process of partnership between you and your coach that uses active listening and powerful questioning to help you explore, dig deep, and move forward to your desired results.

In Christian life coaching, the Holy Spirit works through the coach and the client-coach relationship to call forth what God has placed in you.

I am a professionally trained life coach as well as a John Maxwell Team founding partner and leadership coach. I adhere to the ethics set forth by the Christian Coaches Network International and the International Coach Federation.

It would be my honor to work with you. To learn more about my coaching services visit: https://debbielux-ton.com

More for Your Thriving Life

Articles

Articles are written regularly to bring awareness, help women grow and always to live the thriving life God intended.

Consistent blogging takes place at www.debbieluxton.com/blog

eBooks

Choose to Fulfill Your Legacy, an ebook available at: http://www.onelifetothrive.org/free-offer-sign-up/

8 Tips to a Foundation of Serenity, an ebook available at: https://www.debbieluxton.com

About the Author

Debbie is a very grateful wife, mother, grandmother, daughter and more. She, just like all women, wears many hats. She has been married to her soulmate for 26 years (as of this writing) and together they have five beautiful children. She currently has 10 grandchildren and one great-grandson.

Debbie has 35+ years coaching, mentoring and leading individuals and teams; corporately, in volunteer capacities and in her own businesses.

Debbie is retired from a successful 30-year Fortune 500 Corporate career. In 2010, she started Debbie Luxton Coaching offering individual life coaching and retreats. In 2011, she became a John Maxwell Team Founding Partner and certified leadership coach.

Debbie is the Founder and CEO of One Life to THRIVE, LLC. One Life to THRIVE offers retreats and community for women who are called by God to lead.

"Startups" have always been a part of Debbie's calling. In the Corporate world, Debbie excelled in team integration and the building of new teams. Her experience in this area continued in a volunteer capacity as she and her husband helped lead the startup of the Celebrate Recovery Ministry at their church. Roles they both continue to serve in, now 12 years later.

About the Author

Debbie served on the Missouri Recovery Network Board of Directors; the executive team and leading the organizational development committee as they became a state-wide non-profit.

Debbie served on the Board of Directors for the St. Louis Chapter of the National Association of Professional Women; helping establish this Chapter. She is once again serving this organization as the Community Outreach Director.

Debbie is passionate to help strong-willed, high-achieving women eliminate the unnecessary and focus on the mission critical; God's plan for their life.

Debbie began her retreats in 2010 hosting them in the Ozark Mountains of Missouri. In 2015, Debbie was led to a new location; Colorado Springs, CO. She refers to her retreats as "royal" for 3 reasons: God is "royal" and it's Him we serve, each woman is "royal" as she is created in His image and the location is "royal" as it's at a castle!

As an author, in addition to this publication, Debbie has contributed to 3 books, authored 3 women's retreat studies and authored several eBooks.

References

Alder, Sharon L. n.d. "Shannon L. Alder > Quotes > Quotable Quote." http://www.goodreads.com/quotes/760778-every-woman-that-finally-figured-out-her-worth-has-picked.

Batterson, M. 2011. *Soulprint: Discovering Your Divine Destiny.* Random House, Inc.

Warren, Rick. 2012. *The Purpose Driven Life: What on Earth Am I Here For?* Zondervan.

www.ingramcontent.com/pod-product-compliance
Lightning Source LLC
LaVergne TN
LVHW021342080426
835508LV00020B/2085